P9-DHH-595

"A most accessible text, this work introduces the reader to a wide variety of cultures, enabling you to understand that divinity is a universal concept."

— Rev. Paul V. Beyerl, author of *The Master Book of Herbalism, A Wiccan Bardo* and *A Compendium of Herbal Magick.*

Dancing With Devas

Devas are the semi-divine elemental entities of Spirit, Earth, Air, Water and Fire. Each element has specific correspondences with the directions, moon phases, astrological signs, plants, animals and attributes. And each elemental—and the benefits and powers they bestow—can be accessed directly by various means, methods and techniques.

Trish Telesco is an internationally known writer and lecturer on alternative spirituality in theory and in practice. She is the author of dozens of books ranging from brewing to folklore. Her articles have appeared in *Circle Network News, Fate* Magazine, *Silver Chalice* and *Four Winds Journal.* All her efforts are the foundation of a positive spiritual path. She is a trustee for the Universal Federation of Pagans, a professional member of the Wiccan-Pagan Press Alliance, and an Ordained Minister.

"Trish Telesco is one of the best known writers in her field. Not only is she extremely knowledgeable, she also knows how to relay that knowledge to her readers. There are folk tales, ancient (and not so ancient) customs and beliefs, myths and legends concerning each element. There are also visualization and meditation exercises, rituals and spells, holidays, deities, and so much more for each element. **Dancing With Devas** *is a 'must have' book."*

— Steven R. Smith, author of *Wylundt's Book of Incense*

Dancing With Devas

Connecting with the Spirit and Elements of Nature

Trisch Telesco

Author of *The Urban Pagan,*
Kitchen Witch's Cookbook, Goddess in My Pocket

Belfry Books

Dancing With Devas by Trish Telesco
Copyright©1998 by Trish Telesco

All rights reserved. No part of this book, either in part or in whole, may be reproduced, transmitted, or utilized in any form or by any means, electronic, photographic or mechanical, including photocopying, recording, or by any information or storage retrieval system, without permission in writing from the Publisher, except for brief quotations embodied in literary articles and reviews.

For permissions, or for serializations, condensations, or for adaptions, write the Publisher at the address below.

Painting used in cover art is "Dancing With Devas" by Brian Keeler, ©1997Brian Keeler, PO Box 397, Wyalusing, PA 18853.

Illuminated Alphabet by Kama Lee, 10 Salena, Bentlyville, PA 15314 ©1998 by Toad Hall, Inc.

Production cover and interior pages designed by Steven Dale, 1998, 23420 Happy Valley Dr., Newhall, CA 91321.

Elemental drawings Copyright (c) 1998 by Collen Koziara, 424 East Illinois Street, Wheaton, IL 60187.

First Printing November, 1998
ISBN: 0-9637498-6-2

Published by

Belfry
Books

Toad Hall, Inc.
Rural Route 2 Box 16-B
Laceyville, PA 18623

(717) 869-2942
FAX (717) 869-1031

Dedication

To children and mystics everywhere
whose vision embraces the worlds
we but dare to dream about

Table of Contents

Painting by Brian Keeler, "Dancing With Devas" ©1997

Foreword
An Element-ary Primer

"Do you believe in fairies?"
— James M. Barrie, Peter & Wendy Ch. 13

n beginning any journey, it is always nice to know ahead of time what tools or techniques might be needed along the way. While the most important component in any metaphysical adventure is always you, there are a few methods mentioned throughout this book that you may wish to practice before trying more advanced processes. This chapter is designed to give you the fundamentals necessary for that practice. Adept readers may wish to skip this section altogether, but reviewing it quickly may offer a few new twists or techniques for your consideration.

First, you will need to begin keeping a magical diary. I heartily recommend this practice to anyone studying a spiritual path, not just those reading this book. The magical diary (sometimes called a Book of Shadow or a grimoire) logs procedures and ideas that work for you, which ones do not, and those that you might want to explore later. It is a place that you can scribe your innermost feelings about the divine, devic, elemental, and mundane worlds, and how all these dimensions relate to, and affect, you.

Once started and maintained with due diligence, the magical diary becomes a valuable measure of your learning. I almost guarantee if you read it from beginning to end, about once every three to four months, you will be amazed at how much you've grown, changed, and matured—no matter your physical age or amount of magical expertise. Additionally, the childlike wonder of magic often pours itself into this format when we, in our adult worlds, might otherwise feel awkward in talking about it. This exploration of the inner-child will prove invaluable to your work with the elements and elementals.

Next in order of importance is a basic understanding of meditation and visualization. People getting their first tastes of metaphysical procedures sometimes find the concept of either quite daunting. It need not be so. Translate the idea of meditation into deep contemplation on one specific topic, and visualization into a kind of exercise for one's imagination, and suddenly they seem far more "user friendly."

The basic component to all meditative techniques is breath. Using a slow, rhythmic pace — in through the nose and out through the mouth — helps encourage stress release, calms one's thoughts, and improves overall awareness. I recommend a three count on both inhaling and exhaling as a starting point for practicing this, but eventually you will find a comfortable pace for yourself that is quite natural. As a side note, paced breathing is an excellent way of reigning-in an overheated temper too, which is why we're told to count to ten when we're mad. Breath has the inherent capacity to bring our mind-body-spirit back into harmony.

Once you feel comfortable with rhythmic breathing, the next step is to sit in a comfortable position somewhere private where you won't be disturbed for the duration. Try to have your back well supported, and close your eyes. Breathe in whatever cycle is comfortable for you, and let all the tensions from the day drain slowly away. Now, think about one (and only one) concept or question that has been elusive to you. Keep breathing as you ponder, focusing your mind wholly on that subject. Try not to let your thoughts stray (by the way, this is the hardest part to master, so be patient with yourself).

Keep your magical diary close at hand in case any new insights or perspectives come through. Generally, it is good to start meditating for five to ten minutes at a time regularly (twice a day if possible) then slowly expanding the amount of time to 20 minutes. For example, when you have successfully stayed focused on your subject three times during the five to ten minute meditation, add two or three minutes more. Continue increasing your meditation's time in this manner until you reach the 20 minute (or so) level. This process slowly retrains your mind to hone its operations to your will, and stay attentive to specific matters. This ability is valuable not only for magic, but in every portion of life when you really need to focus.

By the way, don't just stop your meditation/visualization suddenly because you've reached the 20 minute mark (or any pre-determined goal). Wait until you feel finished and give yourself a little extra time to return to a normal state of awareness. Otherwise I can promise you will get a terrible headache!

Adding visualization into this procedure is actually not as difficult as you may think. Sometimes images naturally flow from focused thoughts, but even when they do not this doesn't mean you can't learn to construct positive, helpful portraits. The best way to approach this is to pace the visualization just as you paced your meditations, slowly building the imagery in your mind.

Wait until you've been meditating on your chosen subject for several minutes and feel really centered. Next, the easiest visualization for most everyone to practice and master is that of colored light. Choose any color of light and imagine it pouring down over you like a vibrant summer sun. See how it sparkles with energy. Once this picture is fully formed in your mind, envision the same light filling you, flowing through your pores into every cell of your body.

Breath of the lightlike air. It tingles as it goes through you, picking up any tensions, sickness, and anger along the way. It then leaves from your feet, appearing somewhat muddy. Repeat this visualization until the light that enters your head and that which leaves your feet is the same shade. You should now feel totally rejuvenated, focused, and fairly stress free for working on more specific meditations/visualizations.

For more detailed visualizations, the first step is determining the goal of your meditative time. For example, if you want to find an effective way to settle a difficult argument, you may wish to visualize white or blue light (colors of peace) surrounding you while you meditate. Or, perhaps you will visualize a dove of peace coming from you to the other person involved, thereby opening the door for peaceful discussions. Another alternative still is to find one symbol (like the peace sign) that reflects the theme of your meditation, stare at it for a while before beginning your breathing, then close your eyes and see it within yourself. This helps internalize that attribute.

The exact form and detail visualizations have varies from person to person. Some people imagine a paint brush sweeping over the darkness in their mind, highlighting their chosen imagery. Others observe the darkness as a chalkboard then write upon that board with the chalk of their imagination. Others still, with more vivid imaginations, can simply see full, three dimensional scenes if need be. However, the number of people adept at the latter is relatively small, so don't feel disappointed if you find working with simple symbols or light-forms easier. What's most important here is that you are comfortable with the process. Otherwise you will be expending so much energy on making the visualization work, that it defeats the purpose.

The third item discussed herein regularly is that of ritual. The purpose of a ritual is to create a sacred space within which energies can be raised for specific purposes. Rituals also offer us a physical means of marking and honoring natural progressions in the seasons and distinctive transitions in our lives.

Because humans are creatures of habit, rituals are part of our everyday lives, whether or not we acknowledge them as such. Most people follow a morning routine, take the same streets to work each day, use the same coffee cup, and so forth. In a small way, each of these actions has ritualistic overtones. The major difference between these activities and those of a magical ritual are the setting, intentions, and the respect with which one approaches the rite.

The preparation for, and actual construction of, rituals is highly personalized or dictated by one's magical tradition. However, there are some fundamental parallels including:

• Personal cleansing to release any negative energies that might impede the working. Two examples include taking a ritual bath with herbs, and smudging with incense.

• Personal preparation time, as in prayer or meditation, to bring one's mind-body-spirit all into accord for the purpose at hand.

• Creation of sacred space, frequently by invoking the powers which abide in Earth, Air, Fire and Water.

• Welcoming of a god or goddess figure, either of which may be chosen specifically for the theme of the magic circle. For example, a ritual on Valentine's Day for improving love in one's life might request aid from Aphrodite or Cupid. If a divine figure is called upon, this act may be followed with appropriate libations and offerings to honor that Entity.

• A central activity that builds energy to empower the goal of the gathering. Types of activities include song, dance, music, ritual theater, spells, guided meditations/visualizations, and thematic readings, just to name a few. Again, the chosen activity will mirror the objective of the ritual in some way. Returning to the example of love, the chosen music might be passionate opera to inspire the right mood.

• Releasing the energy to begin its work. This comes near the end of the ritual, sometimes marked by a loud noise, or a key phrase spoken by a leader. No matter the approach, magic will do little good if you don't release it. Remember that it will be necessary to guide the energy out of the protective sphere you've built.

• Closing rites. This is basically a time of thanks and farewells to the powers brought into the circle. If done in a group, fellowship usually follows along with some light food to ground the participants.

• Following up ritual with viable mundane efforts that provide the universe with opportunities to begin manifesting the energy created.

Rituals do not have to be long and complicated, they only have to be meaningful to you. For example, each morning I light a candle, welcome the Powers, whisper a brief prayer for the day while lighting appropriate incense, then say goodbye before going to work. This isn't fancy, but it puts a whole different tone on my day than if I hadn't taken time out for the sacred.

In a world full of rushing, daily, weekly or even monthly rituals like this one become very important. They allow us to stop for one moment and reconsider our place in the universe. Rituals also encourage thoughtfulness in regard to living reciprocally with the earth, peacefully with others, honoring our traditions, and venerating our vision of Spirit.

The fourth technique applied in this text is that of spellcraft. In many ways, spells are mini-rituals designed to meet specific day-to-day needs. Unlike ritual, however, spells may or may not be cast within a Sacred Space, and may or may not call upon divine or devic energies for assistance. Much depends on the spellcaster's philosophy.

For the purpose of having unhindered, controlled energy, it never hurts to set up a protected magical sphere before performing a spell. However, when expediency or your local will not allow that much detail, I recommend visualizing yourself in a sphere of white light until after you release your magical energy. This creates a small, warded region that is a make-shift substitute for the magical circle.

The diversity of spells available from a historical perspective is pretty impressive. Our ancestors were very inventive and insightful in their spellcraft, often turning to those things they used regularly for components. A housewife might draw a dove in her pie crust, then smooth out the dough to encourage "smoother" feelings in the home, for example. A gardener, while pruning the roses, might toss a few petals to the winds with a wish for love. No matter the components or procedures, the purpose of a spell is to focus our minds and spirits on one goal, and put energy toward that end.

Many spells may be changed and adapted to better suit your personal needs and ideology. If you do choose to make personally meaningful adjustments, however, make sure to maintain a congruity of symbols. If, for example, the original spell was designed for love and you want to cast it for health, any component associated with love needs to be replaced with those whose energies amplify well-being. Every portion of a spell needs to be designed so it harmoniously interacts with your intention.

Spells may be repeated at any time you wish to reinforce the magic and encourage manifestation. Additionally, spells should be followed up on a mundane level with viable, personal actions through which the universe can work. Our partnership with Spirit is always a 50-50 proposition. For example, if you cast a spell for a meaningful relationship, don't sit home waiting for someone to show up on the doorstep. Go out to interesting places or participate in activities that you enjoy. The more you do this, the more chances the universe will have to answer your magical request.

The fifth approach discussed herein is that of calling upon divine figures for blessing and consecrating our efforts, thereby sharing positive energy to help manifest our magical goals. Whether you call the force behind life the Great Spirit or the One, by any name this energy is part of every bit of magic ever created. The way in which one connects with and communicates to the divine is very personal. Some may pray, others meditate, others yet sing or write their worshipful phrases. Whatever your personal choice, find an aspect of this Being to whom you can relate, and upon whom you can call to focus and direct your efforts. For one thing, a little outside help never hurts. For another, part of living a magical lifestyle is the hope that someday we can return to oneness with that Power; e.g. obtain enlightenment. However, it is difficult (if not impossible) to emulate that which one does not know intimately.

Finally, the last method discussed is that of contacting and connecting with the elementals and devas that abide therein. Specific, step-by-step instructions are given for this in the remainder of the book so I won't repeat them here. However, please realize that I personally consider working with the elements to be of primary importance to understanding magical principles. Working with devas has tremendous benefit, but should be approached with a very respectful attitude knowing these are semi-divine entities.

All the arts lose virtue against
the essential reality of creatures going
about their business among the equally earnest
elements of nature

— Robinson Jeffers; "Boats in a Fog"

Chapter One
Just the Elementals

An elemental force is ruthlessly frank
— John Conrad

he word "element" has some interesting liguistic connotations. The primary definition is the four substances that constitute all physical matter. Secondary definitions include a basic quality, any substance that cannot be separated into different ones except by radioactive decay, and the first principle. Religiously, the bread and wine of communion are also called "the elements."

These explanations for the term "element" give us much to ponder. From a spiritual viewpoint, if the elements are part of all physical matter, then they are likewise part of us and part of

1

the divine (the "first principle" of creation). Since the elements are also basic qualities, then each person and each facet of the divine has an elemental correspondence to which we can look for more meaning. For example, a flighty person or a god/dess who rules the winds might rightfully both be considered having "Air" characteristics (see later this Chapter).

Additionally, the elements are immutable—even as the spirit or soul of humankind is believed to be immutable. Both may change form, but the basic matrix of what makes up an individual's soul, and each element, always remain the same. To illustrate: earth can become mud, water can become ice, but both can return to their former state. A person can also transform, especially in their roles, yet the essence of who they are (and were) as a spiritual being, does not change. It is part of them like a fingerprint.

Finally, from the delineations provided by Webster, we see that the elements offer us a unique opportunity to commune with the divine. While the exact form of this communion for you may not bear any resemblance to the traditional Christian rite, it is no less sacred or holy. When we work with the elements we are touching, in some way, a part of the universe, the god/dess, and each other.

What's What

It should be noted at this juncture that different cultural settings sometimes describe the elements in different terms, like "wood" and "metal" as occurs in Chinese tradition. For the purpose of this book, however, we will be reviewing the four pre-dominantly noted elements of Earth, Air, Fire and Water, alongside the additional element of Spirit-Ether-Void given in some Eastern philosophies. Effectively this creates the pentagram; a five pointed star in which you, the seeker, stand in the center using your will as a tool for learning and magic.

Of all the elements, Spirit is the most elusive.

Each element has specific correspondences with the directions, moon phases, astrological signs, plants, animals and attributes. All of these will be detailed in the chapters that follow. As a brief introduction, however, Air resides in the east and is an element of thought, learning and movement. Fire resides in the south providing energy, passion and drastic transformation. Water stands in the west, becoming the emotional and intuitive point. Earth is in the north, representing growth and foundations.

Of all the elements, Spirit is the most elusive, residing in the center of All, within and without All, and having no physical quantification. Unlike the other elements that we experience at least partially through one or more of our senses, the only experience we have with Spirit are those provided by faith, and by looking deep within ourselves for that connection.

People are sometimes surprised to discover that they instinctively know more about the elements than they initially expected. Here is one exercise that I like to give to my students to help them become more aware of, and secure in, their instinctive elemental reactions:

Element Identification Test

At random choose three fruits, three vegetables, three flowers, three kitchen spices and maybe one or two trees. Make a list of those chosen. Now, look at each one on the list. If possible, try to experience the item with all your senses. Please make sure you're not allergic to any of these, and that the flower/tree part is edible for experiencing the sense of "taste".

After examining, touching, smelling and tasting, what predominant factors come immediately to mind? For example, with watermelon I find the sweet juice always seems significant, leading to an association with water. Similarly, the pungent flavor and aroma of garlic seems to indicate an alignment with fire. Both of these associations are traditionally correct.

Either mentally or on paper note those factors. Also take a moment to breath deeply and meditate on that item to see if your inner sense gives you any more clues. Finally, write down your best guess at what element each item represents, then check those items in this book or others with good corollary listings (like Cunningham's Encyclopedia of Magical Herbs).

Don't be too disappointed if you get Air or Spirit associations wrong. These are the hardest elements to determine, but most people will guess Fire and Water correspondences correctly. Why? Because in the genetic code of humankind, our early experiences with the elements are still "remembered" in some form. We call this memory "instinct," but it is also an ancestral legacy carried by each cell of our bodies. By using our internal and external senses we tap into this well of information and express it in our awareness.

According to metaphysical theory, elemental beings reside within each one of the aforementioned elements, with Spirit being either an exception to this, or a common meeting ground for all parties. Sylphs command the air, looking much like the traditional fairies of lore. Undines (mer-creatures) command the water. Gnomes care for the earth and salamanders live in fire, among other elemental creatures discussed later by section.

The elementals are intimately connected with the earth's energies, and specifically the matrix that becomes their element of residence. Most folklore indicates that elementals cannot wander far from their base element, or they will cease to exist. It is uncertain from these writings if, at this point, the deva's energy simply returns to its fundamental element, or goes elsewhere.

Elemental beings live in a dimensional plane parallel to ours that is far more etheric and normally invisible to the naked eye, which also explains why logical-minded people have trouble relating to such concepts. Etheric entities find it much easier to shift in and out of our perceived reality, bearing closer resemblance to a light wave than to physical matter. This form rarely stops young children and psychics from seeing them anyway! When these wonderful moments occur, the human mind assembles the flow of energy encountered into the most logical, natural form. Thus, while the names for various elementals change depending on the setting, the imagery seems strikingly similar.

What children and psychics have in common that helps with this perception is a more open crown chakra. When babies are born, they have a soft spot directly over this energy center, helping to maintain their contact with the astral/divine realms. Among psychics, healers and holy people alike this manifests as the nimbus, or halo effect so often depicted in classical art.

So at least one key to improving your elemental awareness and ability to see beyond surface reality resides in learning to work with the crown chakra along with the third eye, the psychic center. Here is one exercise that helps me:

Chakra Cleansing & Energizing

Get into a comfortable sitting position in which good posture can be maintained with minimum concentration. Next, take a moment to relax each part of your body, allowing all the tensions from the day to drain away. Breath slowly and evenly as you do this until you feel yourself moving into a balanced, centered mindset where anything becomes possible.

Visualize a clockwise light swirling on top of your head and over your third eye. These are the energy centers. Don't anticipate what color they may be. While some books indicate a color for each chakra, I believe this changes depending on one's culture, mood, and numerous other factors. Do, however, make a mental note of how the center appears. Is the light murky, muddy, or moving sluggishly? This is an indication that it needs cleansing.

Now, from above you envision a bright sparkling light that first pours into your crown chakra and then radiates through your entire body. Allow the warmth and safety of that light to engulf you. Breath of it as if it were air. See it as blood in your veins.

Notice that as the light moves through the crown region, it purifies the swirling light there, then pours out from your third eye, cleansing that spot too. When you can see the two energy centers as being clear and moving at a harmonious pace, you've completed the first step.

To open and close these points takes more concentration, and some caution is prudent. You don't want to just throw open your home's doors and windows to any passers-by. Likewise, you don't want to open your psychic self to random energy. So, take a brief moment to invoke protection from your personal deities, then visualize a small opening appearing in the center of both chakras, no larger than a pencil tip. Once you can see this, stop! An awareness of new dimensions and energies should be taken in baby steps so integration occurs.

Make notes of how you feel for the next three months after doing this exercise, specifically in how much new insight you gain with regard to the elements, their uses, and characteristics.

This meditation may be repeated any time you feel your psychic self shutting down, or lacking in clarity.

Cleansing and opening the crown chakra is only one step to successful Devic contact. One must also open their heart chakra, the third eye (the psychic center), and learn how to effectively extend their spiritual senses. In a world where we have been taught to perceive all things in concrete terms, opening our inner eyes to discern such creatures usually takes far more than one or two exercises, unless you have a latent knack. For some people, especially linear thinkers, it may even take years of sensual retraining. So try to be patient with yourself.

Remember that one may work with the elements without ever meeting an elemental, and still be very successful in their magic. Also, by working with an element and honoring it, you are likewise working with and honoring the elementals who abide there, whether or not you ever encounter them more directly.

Power Elements And Elements Of Personality

Science delineates animals by their predominant habitat. Aquatic creatures live in the water, for example. Since human beings live on the land, we might be regarded as Terrestrial. Yet, despite our intimate connection to earth, every person I have ever met has one key element to which they strongly respond, and this element is not always Earth.

This key is what I call a power element. To illustrate by way of generalizations, people who love to stand in the face of a rushing wind, or who cannot sleep during wind storms are empowered by Air. People who perk up in hot, dry weather and who seem ever the figurative pyromaniacs are energized by the Fire element. Individuals with Water as a power source find solace in a sea shore and immense energy in water falls. Earth people love to work the land, and have eternal green thumbs.

The elementals are intamately connected with the earth's energies.

Magically speaking, recognizing this element is very important. It can help motivate positive energy for manifestation in your ritual and spell work. For example, my power element is water. So, when I perform auric cleansings for people, the visualization of a light-wave moving through me seems very effective, cresting at the areas of greatest need. Some of the folks I treat actually report hearing waves or feeling like they were in water. Whenever I use this approach, the effort drains me far less.

Additionally, when I'm tense, weary or out of sorts, I find the imagery of being washed by waves very helpful to my personal well-being. The water visualization seems to smooth out the anxiety, increase my energy and return my auric field to a more balanced state. I believe, from talking to other people, that using visualizations like this with your own power element will prove similarly helpful to daily maintenance of body, mind and soul.

Another good illustration is using a power element to build magical energy.

Elemental Energizing

First, think of one spell that you've wanted to try, and one that is fitting in terms of your power element. Healing spells, for example, are more effective with water than air or fire, money spells work best with earth, and so forth.

Next, stand in the center of something that represents your element. For example, if your element is Water, stand on a towel that depicts waves, in a bucket of warm water, or surround yourself with blue-green items. Make sure you have all the items you need to work the spell with you at this juncture.

Center yourself in whatever manner is appropriate to your Path. Release anxieties and focus your mind totally on the energy of the element in which you stand. Feel its energy slowly resonating around and within you.

When you feel like you are wholly in harmony with that energy, begin drawing it into yourself from the ground upward. If it helps, visualize the elemental energy as a color of light appropriate to that element (e.g. Water—blue/green/indigo; Earth—brown/dark green; Air—yellow/white; Fire—red/orange). When the energy reaches your heart chakra (the center of your will), release it with your spell and watch the results. Most people report this method improves their success and again requires less personal energy, having drawn

10

on the elemental levels first.

It should be noted that a person's power element is not automatically the strongest element in their personality. In fact, quite the contrary seems to hold true, perhaps to encourage more balance. For example, thanks to some friends I recently realized that my personality element was Air, because of my propensity for networking and communication. This never occurred to me before, and to be honest it came as quite a shock. Now that I've had time to assimilate the idea, however, it makes perfect sense,

Honor all aspects of nature in word and deed.

and the knowledge has been quite helpful in refining the ways in which I communicate. Now instead of going against the "wind" I move with it, allowing that energy to carry my words. Finding your personality element, and recognizing that of others, will allow for similar positive adjustment in your life.

Discerning Personality Elements

Someday when you have about thirty minutes or so of undisturbed time, gather some paper and a pen and go to a private place. Spend five to ten minutes of your time meditating about yourself: your likes, dislikes, favorite arts, hobbies, annoyances, etc. When you're done, breath deeply and read over the list you've created. What themes emerge?

•**Earth** people often have hobbies like gardening or hiking (e.g. being with nature). Earth personalities are often annoyed by the proverbial gypsy spirits who seem to fly hither and yon without any foundation. Earth personalities frequently like the colors of green, brown and black. Mind you, these are generalities but you see what I mean. Here are some other characteristics that may help you discern your personality element:

•**Air:** Enjoys travel, adventure, freedom and/or athletic endeavors that require movement. May be soft spoken with periodic outbursts. Favorite colors are yellow, white or pastels. Wears light, airy fabrics, and dislikes people who are rigid and overly concerned with rules.

•**Fire:** Has tons of energy but a tendency to overdo everything. Boisterous, sometimes loud, intense presence and a good motivator. Favorite colors are red, orange and bright blue. Dislikes wishy-washy people who can't seem to take a stand. May enjoy saunas, tanning, building bonfires, etc.

•**Water:** Tends towards gentility and being the proverbial "mother" to everyone. Favorite colors are blue, purple and sea greens. Dislikes hot headed people who show no personal control, and also dislikes conflict. Hobbies may include swimming, fishing, and boating.

If you have time at the end of this exercise, it's interesting to detail out a few of your friends and family members. What elemental personality do you seem most drawn to regularly? Keep this in mind as you meet new people.

It is important to note at this juncture that your impressions of the elements may come via sensual input.

A **Fire** person may make you feel physically warm, or perhaps you can actually hear their aura crackling, smell a smoky aroma in the air, or see dancing flames in the auric field. In terms of the other elements, here are some of the sensual cues you may receive:

Earth: rich browns or greens predominant in auric field, smell of fertile soil or meadows, sounds like rhythmic drumming or those that come from an uninhabited forest, feeling is that of cool earth on your palms or grass below your feet.

Air: yellow and white predominant in auric field, smell of a spring breeze, or a freshly opened window, sounds like gusts, tinkling bells, or the rustling of leaves, and feelings similar to that of a wind moving gently over your skin.

Water: blues, blue-green or purple predominates auric field, smell of an ocean, lake-front or after-rain freshness, sounds like waves or trickling water over rocks, and feelings that ebb and flow like the tides themselves.

Knowing your personality element, and recognizing that of others is very helpful to personal relationships, especially when it comes to discussions and improved understanding. Fire people often find themselves quite bitchy around Water and riled up by Air. Similarly, Water people find that Fire personalities can really make them boil, while Air people often provide good motivation. Earth people mingled with Water people makes for muddy relationships, but this also creates the potential for real growth. On the other hand, Earth personalities find that Air people scatter their attentions and tend to uproot well-laid plans.

Again, these are broad inferences, but if you are a "people watcher" you will find they prove themselves out quite frequently. Also, everyone has more than one element that evidences itself in their character. In this exercise we are only discerning the predominant personality element. The underlying elements that periodically intermingle are also what keeps everyone on their toes, and makes each person so unique!

As a side note here, very often people will find it much easier to commune with the deva that abides in their personal power or personality element. This makes perfect sense, considering that you inherently understand and respond to that elemental domain. So, when you first begin trying to contact devas (see also Chapter 2), you may want to begin within your own elemental realm, and slowly extend your proficiency afterwards to other elements.

Attuning To Elements

In the chapters that follow, each element will be examined closely to discern its personality, characteristics, varying historical perceptions, and ultimately its usefulness in our magic. Techniques to help you attune to a specific element are also included in their appropriate section. However, there are some good guidelines to follow before embarking fully on your adventure in element-ary education.

It is important to begin spending more time with nature, both by yourself and with others. When alone, focus on how each portion of nature makes you feel, what thoughts go through your mind, what energizes you, what offers comfort and joy. One exercise that may help you sort this out is the following word association.

Nature's Train Of Thought

For the purpose of this application, start your detailed examination with any outcropping of stones. Use the word "stone" as a starting point on a piece of paper. Next, take a deep, centering breath and write any words or short phrases that immediately pop into your mind as you look at the stones. Try not to anticipate how much you will write, just keep going until you feel done. Review this list afterwards and see what insights it offers you. Keep the information in your diary, you may wish to return to it later for reference.

The progression of words and images in this exercise will be very personal, and relate directly to what you personally need to learn about that object in terms of its element and place in nature. For example, this is what I wrote:

Stone - cool, smooth, strong, durable, water-sensitive, piece of earth's history, cornerstone of elements.

In reviewing this, I learned far more than I anticipated. Despite the hardness of stones, they must give way to water and eventually become earth, even as our soul sometimes must give way to the waters of Spirit for change. Beyond this, stones may have seen memorable moments in history. Perhaps King David walked on them, or Alexander the Great rested thereupon. What wonders we could discover, what aspects of humankind could we learn more about if we but knew how to listen to a stone's story? Now, that's real earth power!

If you found the Train of Thought exercise helpful, try taking it one step further. I recommend arranging something similar with a group of people in the same setting. As each person enters the space, watch how their energy changes and mingles with the surroundings, and how that transformation affects not only you, but also the entire group. Breathing, chanting or singing quietly together usually helps get everyone into the right mental space for heightened awareness before beginning what I call an observation circle.

The Observation Circle

The only two significant differences between the "Train of Thought" application and this technique is that your observations are spoken out loud around the circle, and the additional dimension of having other people's input upon which to build. You may want to have a battery operated tape player handy with which to record the results of this activity.

Have everyone direct their gaze to the stones you studied privately before. If need be, have someone in the group lead a guided meditation to help everyone hone their concentration to focus only on the stones.

After a calm, energy-filled hush falls on the area, the person standing directly in the East of the circle should share the word, phrase or image they receive. The next person, going clockwise, does similarly when person one is finished, continuing in this progression once around the circle. Allow a quite hush to fall once more.

Next, the leader should randomly choose one of the stones and pick it up. This person holds it briefly, allowing their personal element and energies to mingle with that of the stone. They then hand the rock to the next person in the circle who states what differences they feel when they first receive it into their keeping. The second person then likewise allows their energy to mingle with the same stone, passing it on again. This continues once around the circle, and will very often result in a story of sorts, through which you can learn much about the interaction of elements as they are perceived by members of your group.

Once both exercises are completed, take the time to discuss the outcome and any additional insights people might have. Make copies of the tape when time permits so each person can listen to it again at their leisure, and perhaps learn even more!

In your diary, maintain a special section that logs natural observations regularly for at least one year (two years is better as this will show repetitive cycles). Note how slight variations in the weather, barometer, and your own moods seem to affect the energies within and around you. Observe animals and their behaviors before, during and after storms or seasonal shifts. Listen to the voice of a thunderstorm, the whispers of a spring zephyr, and all the signs from nature that gently reflect Divine lessons to our hearts.

Spend time daily meditating on those observations from beginning to end. I can almost guarantee you will be surprised by the insights they offer into your own soul's matrix as it mingles with Gaian energy .

Honor all aspects of nature in word and deed. One cannot hope to understand or effectively work with the elements and devas without this step.

Honoring Gaia

One day when you have a little free time, go to a park or other natural location, taking a pad, pen, and small crystal of your choosing with you (green ones are especially good choices for this exercise). Sit down, relax, and begin enjoying the surroundings. As you relax, focus your attention on the things that you see that may be marring the natural beauty of the location. Don't overlook things like noise pollution, security issues, grease from passing cars, etc.

Make a list of these problems, then note which ones you might be able (realistically) to help with, even if it means just writing a letter to a local politician. Then, commit a small amount of your time each month to following through. Whisper this promise to the crystal you brought with you. Hold it in your hands while visualizing yourself accomplishing those tasks for the Mother. Finally, place this crystal in a tree cleft with your oath. When you have completed the task you set for yourself, retrieve the crystal and meditate with it. See what gifts both the stone and the tree give you in return.

If for some reason the stone is not where you left it, don't feel disappointed. Someone who needed a little earth-energy found it, and now carries your blessing and devotion to nature with them!

Nature is elemental; the devas are nature spirits. There cannot be one without the other. Therefore, the way you think about and act toward the planet and all that abides thereon (including yourself) will have direct repercussions in elemental magics.

For example, When working with and attuning yourself to the Fire element, it quickly becomes apparent that natural fires will work far better for this interaction than chemically enhanced ones. The chemicals can discourage or misdirect magical energy because they do not match the natural matrix. Yes, it is more difficult to make this type of fire, but the rewards are worth your time (and it's far better for the planet too). Beyond taking the old-fashioned approach to fire building, some practitioners even go so far as to gather four different types of wood, specifically for scrying fires, to represent all four elements!

Similarly, when attuning to Water, spring water or other pure sources are a better choice so that pollution doesn't figuratively "cloud" the desired effect. With Air, mingling aromas is fine as long as they are pleasant and positive (versus that caused by nearby factories). If you are a smoker, I recommend abstaining from your habit for a day or so before working with the Air element too. This honors the element and the Earth by your sacrifice (cigarettes do not decompose well), and will also improve your physical capacity for integrating the element (e.g. through breath).

In finding bits of soil or stones for Earth work, choose those that abide in vibrantly growing areas. Nutrient depleted soils, and those heavy with clay, make for rather "dead" energy. Since the soil cannot readily sustain life, magical forces don't move through the former well, and the later tends to hold the energy inside (mind you, this clay does make a good component in healing).

There are some exceptions to these guidelines:

• When you wish to blend Earth and Fire energies (or Water/Earth/Fire) through the use of sand, which would otherwise seem to be unfertile. Again, this should be gathered from an unpolluted beach if possible.

• When you wish to use your energy to promote Earth-healing. In this case having a corrupted element might make an effective symbolic component to your magic, especially if you can cleanse it in some manner.

• When you wish to apply the element to land and garden blessings. Soil can be rejuvenated through the use of natural fertilizer and composting. Add a little metaphysical energy to the equation, and maybe some blessed crystals and tinctures, and the results could be a terrific magical landscape that honors the elements by virtue of your efforts on their behalf.

As one learns to live in reciprocity with the Earth, an inherent benefit is learning about the elements from the greatest teacher we have: nature. As one learns from nature, one cannot help but increase their understanding of the elements! It is a wonderfully complementary relationship that augments not only your daily enjoyment of the simple beauties but also every aspect of your spiritual life.

Spiritual Applications

As I mentioned in the foreword, understanding and working with the elements is of primary importance to successful metaphysical procedures, and our own personal spiritual growth. In considering the "whys" of this, we have to briefly examine the historical role elements have had in traditional magic-making.

Some of our best resources reflecting earlier uses for elemental information come to us from Medieval herbalists and alchemists. Of particular interest are two individuals; Nicholas Culpepper, a renown naturalist and herbalist and Albertus Magnus, an alchemist and mage of much acclaim. Both individuals noted to which element stones and plants belonged, alongside other astrological information. Other period books, whose contents may or may not be totally accurate due to a bias against "witches," also recount magicians working in circles, marking out elemental quarters, and calling upon the Beings who lived within those realms for assistance.

While many of the correspondences listed in the Medieval Grimoires existed long before this juncture, and the writers
of the day were certainly using older sources, the advent of the
printing press suddenly allowed the common person access to
this information. Consequently, some copies of these valuable
treatises still exist for our research today, bearing strikingly
similarity to our own elemental correspondence lists!

Moving forward into a more personal construct, this
means that the attributes and energies assigned to the elements
have been with us for thousands of years. There is tremendous
power in this type of tradition, culminated by belief and repetitive use. What remains for us to discover is exactly how each element works within and around us personally, how to effectively
use the created energy from same, and how *all four* elements can
work together with us, using Spirit as the binding tie.

In healing efforts, for example, you will probably find
that your power element is the one you can use most effectively
in helping yourself or others back to wellness. On the other
hand, certain conditions may lend themselves to the use of an
alternative element, such as a fever being treated with "water"
energies. So, the more adept you can become in working with
each of the elements individually, the more effective you can be
when such situations arise.

Similarly, in terms of personal pathworking, each element offers specific insights and energies to help us. If we only
work with the power or personality element, our mundane and
spiritual lives will always be woefully out of balance, like a table

that's missing three legs! For example, say your personality element is Fire, but you're trying to integrate more patience and peace into your life. These attributes correspond to either Earth or Water, meaning you will have to expose yourself to some of those energies to reach your goal successfully. Such exposure can come through any number of approaches including carrying an appropriate crystal, wearing elemental colors, and filling your home with elemental aromas. The idea here is to change the vibrations in and around your life to mirror the new energy you wish to integrate.

This process does not mean leaving your personality and power elements by the wayside, it simply stretches them (and you) to further levels of understanding so that a blending of elements eventually occurs. In metaphysical traditions, this blending is especially important. As the four corners of creation energize our efforts, guided and empowered by Spirit, suddenly the miraculous becomes possible. In the center of these five points stand we, at the vortex of true magic.

Fairy elves whose midnight revels
by a forest die or fountain,
some belated peasant sees, or dreams he sees
while overhead, the moon
— John Milton, "Paradise Lost"

Chapter Two
The Devas

We are the elves and giants. We are the shining
ones; daughters of the moon and sons of the sun.
— Will Ashe Bason

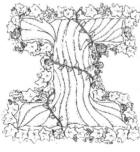
n attuning to an element, you change your spiritual awareness to receive a specific vibration from a widespread thematic source, rather like a broad-band radio signal. This source has definite attributes but no real personification. Consequently one can learn to hear the subtle voice of the elements, but never really communicate with them in the manner that one normally thinks

of for conversation. Conversely, elementals (or devas) are spiritual manifestations that resonate with one specific element and have a clear-cut personality all their own. They can speak, be heard, and exchange ideas just like a person if they so choose.

In truth, these beings rarely take notice of humans unless drawn to them by specific positive energies like love, industriousness, innocence, happiness, playfulness and compassion. Instead of being human-centered, devic entities often attach themselves to a specific place or object, making their presence known only in these locations. When they do decide to make their presence known to humankind, the devas create a very defined signal that may or may not be clearly received and understood by us simply because their vibration is so different from our "concrete" world.

Since the devas do not always want to interact with humankind, the purpose of this chapter is to provide some thoughtful reflections on what elemental beings mean to us in this dimensional reality, and what roles, if any, they should play in our spiritual quest. Please bear in mind as you read this section that I am speaking of "unseen" and scientifically unquantified Beings. Thus a portion of this chapter consists of hypothesis based on the teachings of many ancient, modern and culturally diverse philosophers and theologians.

Elemental Thought Forms

It should be noted at this juncture that some elementals are generated from repetitive, focused thoughts in humans. The energy from these thoughts eventually manifest in the astral. The personality for such creatures are wholly dependent on the thought which created them, one illustration being monsters under children's bed. A very fearful child may actually create their own nightly enemy by repeatedly voicing the ugliness and powers of this creature. There are some modern psychologists who acknowledge that poltergeist activity may be a psychic reaction to physical abuse, for example. Likewise, someone who believes wholeheartedly that a little green man lives in their closet, may eventually manifest that astral being by sheer, consistent faith. This theory gives any responsible magician pause to consider the power of his or her own thought mechanisms.

Another good illustration is the concept of Satan. There is no such being in Hebrew theology, nor in Neo-Pagan beliefs. The visage of Satan was created by the church to put a frightening mask over the nature God known as Pan or Cerrinunos. This aided conversions through fear and misrepresentation. Over the decades, however, this history has been lost. The Church continues to portray Satan as a viable being with impressive abilities. By so doing, they not only invented an enemy but empower his thought-form at every mention of the name!

It may well be that such illustrations give credence to the hypothesis that, if need be, an experienced magical practitioner could design, empower and command a personal thought-form effectively. In minor ways that's exactly what good spellcraft entails when we gather, focus and release energy toward an envisioned goal. Nonetheless, this particular type of engendered elemental is not a true deva per se, and one not easily examined in a book of this nature, as they could potentially be as diverse as humankind's imagination will allow. The information is presented here mostly as food for thought. For the purpose of this book, we will focus our attentions on more traditional elementals as presented in classical beliefs.

Defining Devas

Nature spirits in numerous forms appear throughout the world's mythologies, some being good, others benign, and others yet harmful. In Armenia, for example, the dey are large male or female spirits that are strong and mischievous. Generally they live in caverns and forests (earth centered), and can appear in human dreams as snakes and wild beasts. The only way to protect oneself from their presence is cutting the air with a stick or sword—to cut symbolically their power.

In the Zoroastrian tradition of ancient Persia, the concept of devas took on similarly negative connotations. Here the daeva are demonic-like entities. On a more positive note, in Japan we find the *Marishi-ten*, a Fire elemental who protects soldiers and averts the danger of fires. Similarly, the Benin Earth elementals, called *aziza* (Dahomean for "little people"), dwell in the forest, and generously taught humankind the art of magic and how to worship the Gods in our distant past.

Tibetans have the *Sa-bdag*; deities who are bound to inhabit the place they control. This habitat can be anything from a specific mountain or flower to a person's doorway, a rock, or even a roadway. In this limited respect, they resemble the European fairies that are associated with particular objects or plants, and take on the appearance of those objects/plants. Using this reasoning, a flower *Sa-bdag* or fairy would be very beautiful while one affiliated with a barren field might be ugly or withered looking.

Malaysians believe in the *Chinoi*, a group of supernatural beings who abide in flowers and trees, and aid Shamans in magical workings. This bears some similarity to Native American beliefs regarding the elementals, the Shaman being the one most adept and honing and mastering their energies. In our studies, this is an important point, as Shamanistc beliefs are nature-centered. Thus, before we begin to try working with the devas, we must ourselves return to more shamanic outlooks and awareness.

In Algonquian languages, *manitu* means a supernatural power that lives on and under the earth, and which may manifest to humans if it so chooses. Along the Gold Coast, *mmoatia* are the little people of the forest, equivalent to the *aziza* mentioned above, the *ijimere* of Nigeria, the *apuku* of Guiana, and the *saci* in Brazil. In the United States these beings received no name in the mid 1700s - 1800s, but inhabited the countryside helping industrious humans, and teasing or tricking the lazy ones.

In the Middle Ages, Paracelsus, the Swiss alchemist, described the devas as being somewhere between matter and spirit. Consequently, he felt that the devas could not be regarded as true "spirits" *per se*, because they eat, sleep, have children and eventually die, unlike spirits. Nonetheless they have tremendously long life spans, between 300 and 1,000 years because of their higher vibrational level from the "norm" of the earth plane.

For general congruity, we will be using the concepts of devas based on those portrayed in Indian mythology, and those mirrored by Paracelsus, throughout this text. Here, the word deva comes from a Hindu word that appears in the Vedas meaning "shining one." Such creatures do not exist in the material world, but are instead a force with form.

Consequently, our experience with devas comes far more frequently from inner sight and feelings than it does from physical manifestations. Along the same lines, it is highly unusual for someone in

In Eastern thought, the devas energize and motivate all life.

China to see a deva with European features, and vice versa. As interpreted by our super-conscious, each person's mind translates these forces by clothing them in familiar visages appropriate to their culture. Nonetheless, it is interesting to note that those associated with each element have some strikingly similar features; e.g. Air devas often have wings, Fire devas often appear as flames, Water devas are generally beautiful, and Earth devas are frequently masculine and strong looking.

In Eastern thought, the devas energize and motivate all life, and provide a kind of coherence between the worlds. Like ultrasound uses a gel to resonate and depict images in a comprehensible form, the devas *are* that gel in the broader scheme of things. Theirs is an ancient, sacred pattern which is ever-creative and transformational, but whose center [the realm of Spirit] is constant.

Effectively, devas are aspects of the Earth's energy matrix who have individual thought, characteristics, powers and actions. Some, like the fey of legend are more obvious. Others, hidden neatly in the branches of trees, crevices of rocks, or the patterns on a wind-blown beach are not. Others yet may choose to house themselves in a symbolic object appropriate to their element of choice. For example, a Fire elemental may attach itself to a brazier, lighter, or incense burner.

Tracts of land, bodies of water and winds that seem particularly alive or personified are those inhabited by such beings. These creatures lend an ambiance of magic and holiness to the places where they live. If something bad happens locally, like devastation from war or pollution, the devas will often move away taking their wondrous energies with them. In Sacred Geometry the resulting land mass is called a null space.

Bearing this in mind, these potent earth-patterned personalities hold and maintain the world's mandala, identified modernly as ley lines. By learning to recognize, communicate with, and learn from the devic beings, we will naturally encourage their continued presence and/or return to areas in need. A nice by-product here is also recognizing, communicating with and learning from our own environment. On an extended level, this brings us into a harmonic web with the sacred energy matrix of the universe and the divine.

Elemental Attributes

In European tradition, the Earth devas were called gnomes, dwarfs and trolls. Air spirits are the zephyrs, sylphs and fairies. Fire spirits are salamanders and drakes, and the Water spirits equate to undines and nymphs. But, as seen earlier this chapter, these are but a few names for what is actually a very large, diversified etheric community. Each community of devas has specific functions in the earth plane. Devas also have amazing mystical powers that manifest through their moral and physical attributes. These abilities, however, are intimately linked to the deva's specific element's characteristics and domain. A Water deva, for example, will not be able to perform the same functions and tasks as that of a Fire deva, simply because it is not their element; their basic construction cannot handle "fire" energies.

Within their own element the deva becomes a control system, having the creative power to produce specific effects appropriate to its personality, element, and the requirements of nature. It is important to know these potential effects before you try contacting a deva to be certain the task you ask is possible. Here is a brief listing for your reference:

Air: The power of imagination, learning, creativity, new endeavors and ideas, serendipity, revelation, encouragement, motivation, change, wind magic, whimsy and hope. Indirectly Air also has fertile qualities because it carries seeds.

Fire: Overcoming difficulties or obstacles, psychic and psychological cleansing, mischief, energy and power (be careful here—Fire can warm or burn), zeal, sun magic, protection and purification, drastic transformations that lead to renewal with time.

Water: Intuition and instinct, healing, sensitivity, emotions, cleansing, the ability to flow with life, the maternal nature, generative and fertile forces, psychism, moon magic, and growth.

Earth: Prosperity or other financial matters, practicality, tenacity, constancy, uniformity, cycles, devotion, foundations, Gaia-centered magic, and sensible perspectives or solutions.

> **Bring all your tools, symbols, etc. into the sacred space.**

To put this into a functional vignette, one would probably not call on a Fire elemental to help heal a relationship or open the lines of communication. Water is better suited to such a task, whereas fire might help with passion and forceful communications. Likewise, Air devas can give flight to your dreams and wishes, while Earth provides the solidity necessary for building towards those goals.

Devic Classification

Make a list of personal needs and goals you have at this time on one side of a piece of paper. Now, take a moment to meditate on the devic entities and their attributes as given above. Once you feel attuned to those general characteristics, review the list you made. Next to each need or goal, list the elementals to whom you feel you would go for aid in that matter without looking at the listing again. Afterwards, compare your correspondences with those given. If there are differences, consider why you chose a different elemental personality for that goal/need. In many instances your instincts prove far more important to this work than any guidelines given in a book. Don't automatically dismiss them. Finally, keep this list somewhere safe. As you begin working magic for those needs and goals, return to it as a reference tool to see which deva(s) you may want to integrate into that magic.

Practical Considerations

Before setting up sacred space and trying to contact a devic entity as shown in the next two sections of this chapter, there are some pragmatic helps and hints to ponder. First, make sure you have everything you need to encourage the deva's presence before you begin creating a magic circle. If you do not, stop! Get what you need, and start again from scratch. For safety's sake, do not just idly pick up where you left off.

Secondly, make sure that your personal actions preceding the rite, and motivations for contacting the deva are correct. I find it highly unlikely, for example, that an Earth deva would respond positively to someone who randomly tossed litter on the ground without a second thought just moments beforehand. Likewise, an Air deva might object to being called upon for aid by someone who smokes (see also Chapter 1)!

Third, consider what timing (if any) will help your goal, both for contacting the deva and for the purpose of your behest. For example, folklore often tells of fairies being seen during the full moon, at Midnight and dawn, and on Lammas and May Day, so this type of devic entity might be easier to contact during these dates/times. On the other hand, if your behest has to do with banishing or diminishing, the full moon energies may not be the best choice.

A good astrological calendar is an effective tool in helping to plan the best, most appropriate timing for your devic rituals, should you desire to include this in the equation. This is not a "necessary" step, but it is a helpful one. The more details your rite incorporates, accentuating specific devic energies, the better your chances are of positive results. For example, consider working when the moon is in Taurus, Virgo or Capricorn when contacting Earth devas. These three astrological signs are all associated with the Earth. Astrological correspondences for each element can be found at the end of the chapter for that element.

Fourth, as a protective precaution have a mixture of saltwater, soil, incense and ashes available. Sprinkle a little of this substance around your sacred space to mark the circle and keep the remainder at hand. This blend integrates all four elements, meaning no matter which devic entity you call upon you have the opposite element there with which to banish them. As noted earlier this chapter, not all devas are friendly, nor do all of them take kindly to being drawn into the human domain. This is why I personally recommend *asking* for the presence of a favorable deva, versus *commanding* or *invoking*. The difference in approach is more respectful and frequently more successful.

More information on banishing negative devas can be found later in this chapter.

Fifth, do everything in your power to make certain you will be uninterrupted. Turn off the phone, put a "do not disturb" sign on your door, have someone watch the kids, and consign any undesired pets to another room so they don't cross the circle's energy field randomly. If you are working outdoors, all the better. Natural settings encourage devic visitations far more than man-made ones, and also discourage unexpected guests!

This precaution does not mean that interruptions will totally nullify your efforts, but it will certainly sidetrack them. Should such interruptions occur, I suggest starting your ritual from scratch. This will rebuild the energy and ambiance so your mind and heart recapture that "other world" demeanor, instead of maintaining mundane thought processes.

Finally, consider some type of ritual cleansing before embarking on your rite. This can be anything from fasting for several hours if physically feasible to bathing just before you begin. This action serves two purposes. First, it washes away the everyday life and tensions in favor of a metaphysical focus. Secondly, it cleanses negativity and odd bits of accumulated psychic vibes left in your aura from daily interactions, both of which can misdirect the magical energy you're about to create.

Working Atmosphere

The next step is to create a suitable working atmosphere that will encourage the deva's presence, and put you in the proper state of mind for the work ahead. To begin, just as you cleansed yourself, make sure your sacred space *looks* holy. I have yet to see a dirty church. This doesn't mean your house has to fit into *Better Homes & Gardens*. Just take the time to put things in order so daily tasks don't barrage your senses when trying to concentrate on more esoteric matters.

Find and surround yourself with colors and items that symbolize the elemental upon which you wish to call. This helps attune your spirit to that energy, and also gives the elemental a suitable temporary dwelling place should one decide to answer you. Examples are:

Water: include a cup or glass of water, rice sprinkled like rain, sounds of rain on tape, items that are deep blue or green, and water plants like lilies.

Fire: red or orange candle, brazier, red/orange decorations, a child's fire truck, the stove or fireplace, sand from a desert.

Earth: rich soil or plain stones, a potted plant, a globe, brown and green decorations, roots crops, working in the cellar or while sitting on the ground.

Air: wind chimes, incense, fans, an open window, feathers, yellow and white decorations, working in a high, windy location.

Once you have all the necessary items, the creation of sacred space follows. Attuning to, and dealing with, elementals is a bit different than the general elements. Such entities are creatures of raw drive whose motives are foreign to us. So, in designing your sacred space make sure this is a full, formalized effort that reflects your path and the prevalent needs at hand. Do not skimp on this step. Devas are powerful forces that should be handled with the appropriate preparation. For those who do not have a traditional ritual to follow for creating sacred space, here is one example:

The Devic Circle

1. Bring all your tools, symbols, etc. into the sacred space. Have four areas set up to honor Earth, Air, Fire and Water in the North, East, South and West respectively with appropriate emblems in each quarter.

2. Take a little while to meditate or pray, setting your mind fully on the task ahead. Rid yourself of any lingering tensions, random thoughts about the day, etc. Direct your mind only to the creation of sacred space and contacting this entity.

3. Draw an unbroken clockwise circle of salt mixed with iron filings around yourself, your altar and your cardinal points, leaving enough space within which you can move freely. (Iron is a traditional protective substance against nasty fairies.) Next on the second circuit around, light the quarter candles at appropriate moments in your invocation. Here is one that I particularly like for elementary work:

> *Hail Powers and Residents of the East*
> *Air, fresh with change and motivation*
> *Sylphs who reign the winds*
> *Come join me (us) in this circle*
> *protect the magic as it now begins.*

Draw an invoking pentagram in the air with your hand or a wand. Light the Eastern white or yellow candle to honor the element's presence.

> *Hail Powers and Residents of the South*
> *Fire, burning with energy and emotion*
> *Salamanders who guard the sacred spark*
> *Come join me (us) in this circle*
> *empower the magic; ignite the dark*

Draw an invoking pentagram again, lighting a red or orange candle.

Hail Powers and Residents of the West
Water flowing with insight and healing
Undines whose waters unite the world
Come join me (us) in this circle
manifest the magic; let the waves unfurl

Draw an invoking pentagram, light a purple or blue candle (please note that some traditions have different invoking pentagrams that correspond to each elemental quarter depending on the point where the drawing begins and ends.)

Hail Powers and Residents of the North
Earth rich in abundance, strong in foundations
Gnomes who tend and heal from peaks to sand
Come join me (us) in this Circle
Guide the magic across the land.

Draw chosen invoking pentagram, light brown or green candle.

You may change the wording here so that you show particular welcome the deva to whom you plan to give your behest, and actually I encourage personal modifications so this procedure is more meaningful to you.

4. The third transition around the circle should be to invite Spirit's protection and aid (your personal God or Goddess). As you go, strongly visualize the blinding white light of Spirit connecting each of the four cardinal points to your altar, and a bubble of sparkling energy around the entire working space (e.g. above, below, and on all sides). This visualization and invitation binds the four elements into harmonious balance with yourself as the center point. This effectively creates a protective pentagram that no Being, other than those you welcome, can enter.

Contacting The Deva

Now focus on the elemental of choice. With Water, for example, place some water in your palms and direct all your attention toward that liquid. Try and imagine each molecule of water as a separate, animated being, each of which flows around the other. Feel its texture against your skin as it slowly leaks out to the ground through your fingertips.

Envision a blue-green sphere of light forming in front of you, just over your hands. Continue breathing deeply and concentrating until the sphere feels three dimensional, with a demeanor that is identifiable. This is the first evidence that your attempt is proving successful.

Just before this happens you may notice a change in the air, hear odd sounds or feel differently. (An undine specifically may bring dampness to a room, precede itself with the sound of rain drops, cause the surface of a water bowl to ripple, etc.) Such physical manifestations are the entity's way of saying hello, and it also makes the deva more comfortable in the human environment. Here are some signs that devas from the other three elements may elicit:

Air: Sound of bells or rustling leaves, a wind moving through the room

Earth: Scent of soil or a specific flower, sudden increase in the "density" of items or yourself in the room (a gravity manifestation).

Fire: Increase in room's temperature, candle flame dancing, sun beams suddenly piercing a window and landing in the sacred space.

After you invoke an elemental, detail your goal in a prompt, respectful, precise manner. Do not speak to them as children, and do not order them. To do so is to inspire a very negative reaction from the deva, the result of which can be a really nasty headache. Instead, ask politely explaining your need and why you have requested the aid. Do this by extending both hands in the direction of the devic globe visualized, and direct your request into the globe. A good rule of thumb here is KISS (keep it simple).

> In European tradition, the Earth devas were called gnomes, dwarfs and trolls.

Devas can be impatient, and often dislike idle prattle. Again, the request for the elemental should be chosen appropriately for that Being's known abilities and talents. Each deva may help those of another element, but cannot perform tasks outside their elemental dominion.

It might be very tempting at this point to want to talk to the deva further, or just look at them. They can be stunningly beautiful. Nonetheless, do not make the creature tarry any longer than necessary. Whether or not they agree to help you, simply thank and release them after the encounter. Remember, devas can be temperamental and unpredictable, so its best to finish your work quickly.

If you have a *valid* reason for lengthening their stay, don't hedge the subject. Be totally honest. Ask if they can tarry and tell them why. Don't be surprised if the answer is no; devas have work all their own, let alone the task you've given. If they do agree, however, the interaction can be re-markably enlightening.

Generally devas will communicate empathically or tele-pathically. Water devas flow with emotion, Air devas are a little elusive and sometimes difficult to understand, Fire devas are quite forceful in their opinions, and Earth devas are, well, down-to-earth with their advice! Try not to interrupt their discourse as this is considered an insult (unless you've been fortunate to get a very talkative fey).

Once the deva has expressed its message to you, it will likely want to leave fairly soon thereafter. At this juncture it is time to expediently express your thanks, open a doorway in the magic circle, and allow the deva to pass. Do this by slicing a visual doorway in the energy, then gesturing outward. You will feel the deva's energy move by you, often causing the hairs on your body to raise like with static electricity. When it is outside the circle, close the sphere once more until you're ready to dismiss the guardians.

Now, before you forget the subtle details of what happened, take your magical journal in hand and write it down! Enjoy as much time as you can in this space with the Sacred, interpreting and integrating the experience. Make special notes of the areas of your ritual that you perceived as particularly successful or unsuccessful. These notes will be very useful in designing future devic rituals. Close the circle when you feel ready, dismissing the four quarters with a thankful heart.

Pros And Cons Of Devic Conjuration

Earlier this chapter I spoke briefly about the fact that not all devas are friendly, nor do they always enjoy responding to human requests. Just like humans have positive and negative aspects, the devas have their darker sides, or more difficult personality traits with which to wrangle. Air's danger lies in its ability to go overboard, uprooting and blowing over things thought to be firmly grounded. Air devas are also very changeable and whimsical, like the wind itself, making the outcomes from their efforts unpredictable at best.

Fire's difficulty lies in the fact that it is very hard to control. Without constant tending these devas may rage, burn themselves out, or smoulder away before their work gets done. Similarly, although Water's inherent nature is gentle, it has a fearsome side in typhoons, floods and other type of nature's fury. Water devas are also sometimes a little too pliable. Having no defined form than that provided by their environment, they may manifest your wishes very differently than you anticipated. In other words, the final "shape" of your magical energy will depend on where this deva takes it!

For all its strength, Earth is not without it's shaky aspects. It can be worn away or harmed by each of the other elements, meaning your magic could be deterred by nature's hand. For example, if an Earth deva encounters water in its task, the effort could get muddied up!

These examples potently illustrate why working with the devas is a task to be well thought out. If at any time you feel that the entity you've contacted does not have your best interest in mind, or may have malevolent energies, you have every right (and the wherewithal) to banish that Being. Remember you called them, and this is your sacred space, so you can kick them out of it!

To banish an unpleasant elemental, open a doorway going outward from your sacred space (make sure this is a one-way energy field, like a door that only swings in one direction). Next, take a handful of the salt mixture spoken of earlier in your hand, and either throw it toward or blow it onto the devas manifestation so that you move it in the direction of the doorway created. Bid it to leave using simple words like "leave this place, you are no longer welcome here, and never to return." Once the deva is outside your sacred sphere, close the doorway and continue repeating your command until the entity disappears completely, and all signs of its presence are gone from the room.

If you must banish a deva, I strongly suggest embarking on a regular routine of reinforcing the protective wards you have on your home for a while. Most devas won't bother you after this, but some can get quite persnickety and stubborn, trying to cause a little uproar in your home because they've been rejected. When you protect your wards, sprinkle the salt mixture in a counter-clockwise direction to banish negative energies and keep them firmly outside where they belong.

Symbolic Alternatives

Because of the aforementioned lamentations and difficulties, summoning elementals is not a task with which everyone feels "at ease." Even adept practitioners don't just randomly call on the devas like a servant just waiting to do their bidding. The respect these Beings deserve does not allow for casualness, or callousness. For example, while I have been fortunate to see and experience a few elementals over the years, such meetings were always prompted by *them*, not me, and I have been quite content with that arrangement!

Consequently, for people reading this who are new to magic in more ritualized forms, alternatives to direct contact may prove just as useful (not to mention less worrisome). In this case, you will be directing your desire into something that *repre-*

sents the element in which your desired deva resides, and letting that medium carry your behest.

For example, say you hope to enlist the aid of an Air deva to encourage movement in a situation that seems to be stagnating. One way of accomplishing this goal might be to wait for a gusty day, and then go outside with a leaf gathered from near your residence. Hold it in your hand, focusing totally on that desire, then write the word "movement" on the leaf. When you feel the winds rising with your energy, release the leaf so it carries your message to the devas. Better still, this is an effective spell in its own right for motivation, incitement and change!

Symbolic alternatives readily allow you to combine elemental symbolism to increase the sympathetic magic created. This encourages cooperation between the devic kingdoms to help achieve your goals. Here are some examples.

Prosperity: Take a coin, a seed and a handful of soil and toss it into a Northerly wind [the quadrant of Earth] so finances "grow."

New Job: Take a yellow-colored fall leaf [the color of the mind] as an earth/air symbol [air for the mental, earth for foundations] and float it on a water source moving away from you to smooth the transition ahead.

Health: Burn an emblem of your malady to make it visually break down, then wash away the ashes in water to carry the sickness far away from you and promote bodily cleansing.

Anger: Place a piece of paper detailing the reason for

your anger in a brazier or other fire-safe container. As it burns, squelch the flames with ice or water to likewise cool your emotions. Note that this spell works well for cooling passion too!

Remember, working with the element indirectly allows you to work with the beings who live therein. Never feel this is a less powerful or effective way of working. In the sphere of a magic circle, a symbol is no less potent than what it represents. So trust in yourself to know when you should, or should not, try to work with the devas, and allow that voice to always be your best guide.

Dancing With Devas

Spirit of insight
Font of creativity
Sister Sea
Womb of Diana
We honor thee.

Let the waves of cleansing, healing and intuition flow
to that which is our soul.

Your gentle movements caress the shores of Gaia
feeding, refreshing, then leaving
softly as you came.

Yours is a potent beauty
patiently tending and waiting
until the hardest stone is
honed by your hand.

Yours is also the moon
waxing and waning
with silver droplets that fill
a wanting spirit.

At your shores
unceasing movement reaches ever toward us
salt preserves us
passion crests.

Your voice is the ages
whispering mysteries
calling us homeward.

Chapter Three
Water

rom space, our planet appears like a giant blue marble dotted with white—the oceans uniting the Earth into a sphere that knows no boundaries. Thousands of years ago, the winds of change blew across these waters, and the Wheel of Life began to spin. Out of this churning mass of azure potential came the first signs of life, and the genesis of humankind.

It is therefore no wonder that so many people find themselves inexplicably drawn to the echo of waves against a shore, the roar of a waterfall, the murmur of a river, or the soft splash of raindrops. Water, in all its forms, gently summons us back to our ancient ocean home. But when we arrive at this familiar shore, what lessons await us?

Our earliest ancestors required water for survival, but it was not gathered without risk. Other creatures also needed this precious liquid. And too, sometimes water fell from the sky accompanied by horrible sounds that frightened primitive minds. In reviewing the folklore and mythology of water, this odd dichotomy should be kept in mind. For ex-

49

ample, the same people that once thought traveling too far across the ocean would mean falling off the Earth, or risk being eaten by sea monsters, also believed that water could heal and act as a conduit of Divine blessings.

As time inched forward and humankind developed, the power and potential of water was slowly recognized and honored. Beyond the daily routine of cooking, cleaning and personal care, water was part of nearly every human endeavor. Farmers watched expectantly for rain. Seamen observed the oceans to know when to explore and fish. Townspeople gathered at communal wells to appease indwelling spirits. Travelers carefully gathered fresh water to take on long journeys. Children were baptized in holy water. Healers sprinkled blessed water on patients or threw items representing sickness into running waters. In all of these activities, and many more, the spirit of water nourished and adorned human history in ways we can only begin to imagine.

Mages, religious leaders, philosophers and common people alike didn't overlook this important connection. Socially among the ancient Celts of high and low birth, the cup was a token of hospitality, which is perhaps why one of the first rules of hospitality is offering guests a beverage. Religiously, cups still adorn the altars of various traditions around the world as a symbol of this element. Philosophically, many great thinkers including Paracelsus conjectured that elements surround and intercept the earth as living, intelligent beings. The "bodies" of such godlings are a mixture of spirit and matter, being inseparable from their component element for any elongated period of time.

Metaphysically, water was assigned to the western portion of creation, where creatures like the undines and mythic mermaids personify its essence. Specific correspondences for this element, established by our ancestors, continue as part of the modern magician's working representations. Of these associations, some of the most predominant ones are healing, gradual change, patience, maternal energies, and fertility (see also Correspondence List).

Myths And Legends

Many creation myths and legends include water or the sea as being a prime element in our beginnings. According to Vedic beliefs, for example, before all things there was a dark watery chaos. Then the germ of life, gifted with unity, developed— eventually manifesting itself as the cosmic egg from which the gods, the universe and humankind all originated. Similarly, Egyptians considered the seas as the Father of the Gods, the Babylonians believed the ocean was God's dwelling place, and Mexicans revere rivers as an emblem of the Mother Goddess.

In Assyro-Babylonian mythology, all things arose from Apsu (sweet water) and Tiamat (salt water). Tiamat was the personification of the sea, whose womb birthed the world. She is also the inventive power of chaos. It is not surprising, therefore, to discover that the people of this region regarded water as the instrument of divine justice.

In Samoa a slightly different version of creation says that

51

a primeval octopus emerged from the land. When its ink sac broke, the sea burst forth with all creatures therein. Stories like this and the one from Babylon, previously, lead to this element's association with inventiveness and fertility.

Myths and legends from various cultures also attempt to explain natural occurrences, specifically tides, in unique ways. Teutonic tradition has one of the most amusing anecdotes that tells us of Loki, a mischievous god, placing the end of a drinking horn in the ocean before Utgardalonki challenged Thor to a contest. Upon receiving the challenge, Thor proclaimed that no one could drink as much, or as quickly, as he. Try as he might, however, he could not drain the horn and was terribly embarrassed. Ebb tides remain today as a result of Thor's thirst for victory.

Rain is sometimes explained as angels drawing water into leaky buckets. This particular explanation, by the way, evidences a theme in folk tales about carrying water in a sieve or an improper container. Such a task was often a test of sorts, a punishment, or used as a means of escaping a terrible fate. Only the chaste or true of heart could accomplish the impossible, and truly clever individuals repair the water's holder!

Another ancient natural occurrence, or in this instance a disaster, was the flood. Deluge myths reoccur in many cultures indicating a wide-ranging effect on the human consciousness. Among Assyro-Babylonians, the gods one day decided to destroy the human race by drowning. Ea, a water god, had compassion for humanity and secretly built a reed hut so a few would be saved. Similarly, in South America there is the story of Bochica whose wife was jealous of the attention humankind was getting. So, she tried to drown them, at which point Bochica cleaved the mountains that closed the Magdalena valley to let the water out, saving many lives. These two stories give water the symbolism of purification, drastic change and unexpected mercy.

In some flood myths it is not humankind who rebuilds the earth. In some Caribbean regions, the story goes that just when the last humans were about to die, a water bird brought a basket of soil.

Metaphysically, water was assigned to the western portion of creation.

This bird, with the aid of ducks, began recreating the earth.

Folklore & Superstition

Water has a significant place among the world's folkways. From the earliest writings we find instances where various types of water were honored in diverse ways. The ancient argonauts doused their ships with mead to appease the restless spirit of the sea, for example. In old England, people dedicated the entire month of May to celebrations wherein offerings for beneficent indwelling spirits were left upon sacred wells around the country. On a less pleasant note, if one drank from a haunted stream in Europe, they ran the risk of contracting lycanthropy. Apparently the haunted waters release the "beastly" nature.

Here are some other examples of interesting folk beliefs pertaining to this element:

Blessings
• The Muhammadan prayer beads are often blessed with water by dipping them in the Zenzem well, located in the holy city of Mecca. Local people believe this is the well where Ishmael once drank.

• 12th century Germans blessed their fields by mixing holy water with oil, milk and honey. This mixture was spread upon the land before dawn along with prayers.

• Macedonians splashed water on their courtyards every January 2nd to bring luck, peace and protection from witches for the coming year.

• Water steeped with heather if used for bathing on the night of a full moon blesses the washer with beauty beyond compare.

• Mandaeans were a semitic sect who lived in lower Babylonia participating in the blessing rites of baptism. To them, however, the Christian approach is unthinkable as the water is not "living" (e.g. it isn't from a natural moving source).

• In Wales, people sometimes rose early on New Years day to skim water from a wealthy neighbor's well to "steal" their luck and divine favor.

54

Divination

• One of the oldest forms of divination, originating in ancient Greece and India, was to place blots of ink or wax on water contained in a silver basin and scry for patterns.

• Dousing with a hazel branch up until 100 years ago was called the art of "water witching." This is, in fact, a form of geomancy.

• People in seafaring communities sometimes looked to the time a tide arrived for portends. If it arrived early in the morning it meant a fertile day; by full daylight, prosperity; at midday, tenacity; at dusk, transitions; during the evening, happiness; by night, insight; at midnight, renewed wholeness, and before the first rays of light, leisure.

• Babylonians observed the state and appearance of their rivers for signs and omens.

• In Britany a child's shirt is tossed into water to determine if they will survive an illness. If it sinks, the omen is negative.

• Some cultures believe that the voices of their ancestors can be heard in rushing water, and if you listen closely you can receive their messages of knowledge or warning.

• Among ancient Hebrews, holy water mixed with the dust from the floor of a tabernacle was a way of detecting a curse or sin, especially that of adultery. If a person was guilty, their thighs and belly were supposed to rot upon consumption.

• Unusual forms of rain, those bearing milk, toads or stones, are very negative portents. They precede disasters like fire, invasion, war and earthquakes.

Health

• The Gnostics used water for healing magic, especially in combination with other emblems. For example, to cure disease the charm Abracadabra (which means to perish like the word) may have been written in an inverted triangle on paper then tossed in running water to carry the sickness away.

• Romanian people use a pitcher of water as part of a cure for backache. Here, knots that were tied along the inflicted's back are placed in the water until they can be disposed of in a source of water moving away from the patient.

• An Assyrian cure for headaches is touching a black and white cord to one's head then tossing that cord in running water.

• Water-worn stones were considered by many ancient civilizations as being excellent amulets to avert evil.

• In Scotland, the water used to wash a group of stones known as "stones of victory" was often given to the sick to aid their recovery.

• Rain gathered from the roof of a church had restorative powers according to old English tradition.

• Do not bring snow into the house of an ill person, or they will get worse.

• In Scotland, water mixed with flakes of gold and silver was sprinkled around children suffering from sicknesses caused by the evil eye to disburse the magic.

• Among the Irish it was believed that dew gathered from the grave site of a clergyman can cure disease.

• In England, the dew gathered throughout the month of

May, and particularly on May Day (also called Beltane) grants beauty and good health.

> • In Slavonic regions, water is a Power worthy of worship because of its metaphysical nature. People here wash regularly in flowing water, offering the spirits that abide therein flowers and prayers for health.

> • Rainwater is said to aid eye illness.

Love

> • Lovers who meet near running water insure that their communications will be truthful.

> • Lovers who are rained on coming out of the church will have a long, happy marriage with many children.

> • Lovers who marry during the ebb tide are granted happiness.

> • If you boil water over on the stove it portends the loss of love. If boiling water falls on a rug it portends quarrels.

> • After a wedding, brides should cross a stream and toss a token over their shoulder saying, "bad luck be gone." This keeps good fortune with the couple.

> • If a Celtic couple went to a wishing well right after their wedding, the first to drink from it became the dominant partner for their lives together. Following this, the two would walk clockwise around the well thrice to make a wish.

> • Gaulish tradition says that two people who wash in the same basin of water invite arguments.

Weather

- During times of draught, water is frequently poured upon the ground as a precious offering in the hopes that the divine will likewise be generous.

- In China, tossing jade into sea water is believed to bring rain, mist or snow.

- A twig or broom dipped in water then sprinkled on the ground will bring rain.

- If it rains on St. George's feast day, it is said plums and barley that year will be scarce.

- To turn away storms and change hail to rain, put a cutting implement point upward in the garden, or the face of a mirror. Additionally, put three grains of salt on anything you wish to protect from hail damage.

- Holy water from the Pentecost has the power to avert storms.

- When snow melts slowly, another storm is coming. Yet, a good snowfall is said to protect crops.

- In ancient Greece and Rome, oak was dipped in water as Zeus was invoked to bring rain. In Teutonic tradition, water was poured over a naked girl to bring rain, and in India priests poured water into small holes on the temple floors for similar purposes.

- In some regions animals are considered custodians of the rain, including frogs, toads, snakes and lizards. To bring rain, these creatures are supplicated then sprinkled or dipped in water. If the downpour proves too great, the creature should be gently placed by a fire to dry and kept there until the earth is likewise dry again.

Water Attunement

Before working with any element it is always a good idea to become more familiar with its inherent characteristics. In your own home this process can begin with a long, leisurely bath or shower. While enjoying the warm water, breath deeply and extend your senses. Pay particular attention to the way the water feels against your skin, its scent, and sounds. Make notes of your impressions in a journal.

Next, if possible go to places where you can experience different types of water: a fountain, river, well, hot springs, lake or ocean beach are all good choices. If you have no such areas nearby, wait for a rainy day and go outside. Relax and reach out again, this time silently extending a "hello" to the water. Listen closely to each drop.

Realize that the same water that fell upon Moses still exists in some form as part of the rain, tap water, puddles and moist air that now touches you. That same dew connects you to the Earth's oceans, and the life-giving force of Gaia herself. Think about that connection, try to sense and feel it in your skin, your cells... the very core of your being.

You may notice that after a while the water almost sounds as if its speaking to you. That's exactly why people often use the description "babbling" when they talk about brooks! At this point don't focus too closely on trying to discern exact words.

Instead check your emotional or empathic impressions. Elements often communicate this way, each having a special voice that we can learn to hear with spiritual ears.

Each element also has unique lessons to teach us. Water specifically shows us the power of flexibility by filling any shaped container. It also reveals the strength of consistency by wearing away hard rock a little at a time.

Because of its fluid nature, Water can flow freely to the past or future to give us needed perspectives, but the information may not always be understood immediately. Consequently, be sure to keep notes on all your experiences with, and messages from, this element so you can refer back to them later. Re-read your notes once every couple of months and see what new insights they offer. As you do, remember to attune yourself to the element again first so that your spirit is in harmony with that energy, thereby making any missives clearer.

Water Healing

Except for individuals who may be water-phobic, this element is uniquely suited to the gentleness of healing arts. Mundanely, we already associate water with cleansing, soothing, and fluidity. Metaphysically the deeper associations for these attributes follow suit.

Water healing techniques can be augmented and amplified by working with the appropriate lunar cycle. Since this element is so closely controlled by lunar energies, it may even be considered an "essential" part of the treatment process. That decision is one for the healer to make. Here are some examples:

Dew: Dew gathered at dawn exorcises spells that cause illness and aids longevity. One caution exists. Do not roll in morning dew as this brings on fever.

Fountains, Springs, Wells: Sacred healing wells, fountains and springs dot the European countryside like buttercups. In ancient times, people would give the spirit of the water an offering (like the modern wishing tradition with coins), and then either bathe in the water, pour it over themselves, or leave a piece of cloth hanging in a nearby tree which sympathetically also left the illness "hanging."

Some areas, like Lourdes in France, have very elaborate rituals where the seeker should approach the site from the right hand side, walk around the water three times, then make their

> **Water has a significant place among the world's folkways.**

offering. A modern equivalent for this would be going to an energetic water source like Niagara Falls, gathering and blessing some of the water (perhaps with healthful herbs mingled within), then wash or rinse the affected part of the body. The important thing to remember here is that the water source must be one that is refreshed somehow (not stagnant).

Rain: Among some North American Indian tribes, the

female rain, that which falls gently on the earth, has healthful qualities especially for women wishing to conceive.

Sea Water: Go to the seashore and wash your feet and hands thrice. The remaining water should be poured out behind you. This is an ancient Scottish tradition for banishing the spirit of sickness.

On another level, seawater has a high saline content, making it an excellent healer/cleanser for our magical tools and sacred space. Anything that is not damaged by saltwater can be rinsed or washed with it to negate residual negativity and balance the basic matrix back to normal.

Sprinkling Water: North American Shamans sometimes asperge a patient's aura with charged, blessed water to bring the energy back into symmetry. At home, to empower the water, begin with a base of spring water and put it beneath a waxing moon (for increased energy) or a waning moon (for banishing illness). Also let it absorb some solar rays. The sun is a symbol of divine blessings. This approach should be repeated three times over three days.

Sweet Water: Water that flows naturally pure, like that which is produced from mountain snows, is considered sweet. In the Middle Ages such waters were often part of prescriptions, creating the base for a medicine or becoming the medicine themselves. The additional benefit of sweet water is that it battles the melancholy that often accompanies being ill.

Tears: Our tears are one form of water that many people don't think of immediately. They are potent, having released energy with emotions and bearing a cleansing quality all their own. When someone cries out of concern for you, put their tears in water to drink of their love and let it heal you.

Waves of Healing: Carry a token of your malady with you for seven days. At dusk on the seventh day go to a beach and place the token within reach of the incoming tide. Turn your back, and walk away as the sun sets. The waves will carry the token (and the sickness) away from you.

Additionally, if you wish to help someone far away, you can whisper or sing words of well being into the waves and let them transport your good will to where it is most needed.

Water Meditation and Visualization

For people who are stressed out, or folks who desire a constructive meditation/ visualization that helps purify and balance the aura, Water is an excellent element to incorporate. Since almost everyone has seen a waterfall or other water source, it is easy to visualize this liquid in your mind's eye. As you would for any meditation, however, the first step is getting comfortable and making certain you won't be disturbed for a while. Turn off your phone, put a note on the door, and keep pets in a different room if they're liable to distract you.

After finding a personally cozy position for yourself, begin breathing in a deep, all-connected manner so that the end of one breath naturally flows into the beginning of the next. Make an honest effort to keep thoughts of mundane matters out of your mind. Focus only on the sound of your heartbeat and breathing.

Once you feel really calm and centered, visualize yourself in a welcoming natural setting with a water source. I personally recommend a waterfall, but if you're drawn to a different type of water, use that imagery. When you can see your surroundings in detail, extend all your senses. Can you smell the aura of the water on the air that surrounds you? Can you hear its gentle voice calling? Follow that sound.

In your imagination, walk slowly through this sacred space until you reach the water source. Remove any clothing you wore here one piece at a time, laying aside your worries, your tensions, sickness, any anger, or other negative thought-forms with each piece. Then, reach out to the water and ever-so-slowly immerse yourself therein. This is the depths of the subconscious, it is also a place of total peace and purity. Commune with that energy as long as you wish, then slowly return to normal awareness.

Spirits are very unpredictable, and often fickle.

An alternative to this visualization is using the imagery of a deep, dark cave wherein a beautiful pool filled with watery light dwells. All around the outside of the pool candles are lit awaiting your arrival. The water here has a silky-satiny texture from the light it holds. Imagine the hue of the water as a color that reflects your current needs. For example, if you need to bring peace to a restless relationship, try a pale pink light—the color of friendship. Here are other color correspondences to consider:

> *Yellow*: improve the flow of creativity and inventiveness.
> *Sprout green:* matters of health & healing, finances & fertility.
> *Blue*: peace, rest, easing tensions and worries.
> *Purple:* spiritual meditations, matters of the soul.
> *White:* purity and protection.

As with the other meditation described herein, you may continue in this place as long as you like. You will naturally know when your work there is completed. Don't try to move too quickly after such visualizations, however, as it can undo your good efforts and result in a headache.

Rituals

Water was, without doubt, the earliest liquid to partake in ritual of any sort. Gathered from the sky's tears, a nearby stream or other water source, it was left out as offering to the spirits of nature that later developed into personified gods. The original ritual tools for this precious liquid were as unadorned as they were the human hand, a hollowed-out gourd, a seashell, perhaps half of a coconut. Yet the meaning was not lost to the participants; that of sharing a cherished substance with the creative, substantive All-Power of the universe.

Among modern magical practitioners, a chalice or cup continues to honor the element of water upon the altar. Some practitioners choose to use other symbols, but the connotation is the same no matter the media. In many ritualized settings, it is customary to pour out a small libation of water (or other liquids) to the god/desses of the group (or home) as a way of revering those sacred presences. Additionally, sometimes water will fill the cauldron of a group (or other implement) for asperging, which is a ceremonial cleansing accomplished by sprinkling all in attendance.

If a ritual has been conducted specifically for healing, the perimeter of the circle might be marked by a trail of water to mark the line between world and not-world. For blessing-way rituals performed for babies or young children, the element of Water is shared with them that they may never thirst physically, emotionally or spiritually. This ritual also introduces them to each element as "nourishers" of the human soul.

For handfasting, which is akin to marriage, the couple may share of a single cup of water (or wine) to show their unity and purity of intention. During banishing rituals, Water can become the implement of purification by dispersing it out toward the area in which difficulties are perceived. In effect, since rituals are similar to elongated spells, Water can be used in this setting in the same manner in which it functions for your spellcraft.

Water In Spells

In the correspondence listing, I have provided some generalized topics to which water is an excellent component for spellcraft. Exactly how you design your spells is something rather personal. So instead of giving you exacting instructions for specific spells that may not meet your needs, I have instead assembled this list of how to bring the element of Water into your sacred space for spellcraft, and to what ends that form may be applied:

Dew: Since the days of merry olde England, this has been collected as a beautifier. For magical purposes apply it lightly to your aura to bring loveliness within.

Fog: This is a wonderful time in which to work magic of any nature. Fog gives the impression of timelessness, which is exactly what we hope to achieve in the sacred space.

Ice: To cool heated emotions, or "freeze" negativity and gossip. For example, place the name of the person with whom you're having trouble on a piece of paper in your freezer. Since ice melts into liquid form if left out long enough, it may also be applied to matters where one desires a "decrease" or dispelling like with weight loss or ridding negative habits.

Liquid: All functions of water. Also, if the water is moving, use the direction of motion to bring things into, or bear things out of, your life.

Rain: Rainwater has been used for aeons as part of healing magic, being gathered, blessed, mixed with other ingredients and then given to the person in need. It is also an excellent emblem of nourishment and cleansing.

Snow: Akin to ice in all its attributes, except that no two snowflakes are alike. Use it in spells for originality too!

Sweat: In Iran, sweat has creative properties. Iranian cosmetology credits the creation of the first man to the sweat of Ahura Mazda, a great god. With this in mind, your own body's fluid can encourage manifesting energy in your spellcraft.

Tides: Among the Norse, the timing of each tide was symbolic, and could be used to amplify spells. Midnight tides accented recuperation and well-being, those just before dawn encouraged rest and peace, the noon tide provided strength and tenacity, and the tide at sundown is that of transition and change.

Observances

Early April: Boat Festival in France. Children set small boats adrift on the Rhine with candles within to bear good wishes to the finder.

May (entire month): Sacred well celebrations in England wherein all the wells of the countryside are decorated with offerings for the indwelling spirits. This was an offshoot of the Roman celebration of Fortunaillia which took place on May 26.

Mid May: Rain ceremonies in Guatemala to help bring plentiful downpours and abundant crops.

May 19-28: Ancient Greek festival wherein all the sacred images were taken to streams, rivers and lakes for cleansing and purification.

June 17: Festival of the Cleansing Lily in Japan. This

celebration is designed to stop flooding downpours that often come at this time of year. It features a ritualized gathering of lilies and temple prayers.

Early Summer: Alaskan Whale Dance is done to give thanks to these sea-dwelling creatures for their providence.

July 3: Celtic festival of Cerridwen. This ancient goddess had a cauldron which held a magical liquid that gave anyone who drank wisdom and creativity.

July 25: Tenjin Festival (Shinto). Papers rubbed against the celebrant's skin are given to moving waters so that any sickness can be washed away.

August 1-3: Day of the Dryads in Macedonia. This festival celebrated the devic/spiritual entities who resided in specific plants or natural elements including the water.

September 15: Birthday of the Moon in China. The moon is the strongest influence on the element of water, so this is a suitable holiday on which to honor it.

November 9: Loy Krathong (Thailand). Banana leaf boats get water-launched with candles today with the participant's wishes. If the candle stays lit until the boat is out of sight, local custom says the wish will come true.

Winter, Pre-Spring: Frost Fairs, Ice Festivals and Snow Balls. Dates vary depending on your locality. Great celebrations in which to honor the spirit of water in one of its many forms.

Water Devas And Their Workings

The ancients held that there were many groups of water elementals known as undines. Some lived in waterfalls, others in the mist, others still in rivers, marshes and lakes. Many early people believed that every fountain and well had its own water nymph, and each ocean had an oceanid. Other names for these creatures, often derived from their dwelling place, included oreades, limoniades, naiades, sea maids, and potamides.

Undines get their name from a word meaning wave. These are beautiful water spirits, often appearing female, and they enjoy the company of humans. Lovers, creative people and those with a versatile nature attract an undine's attention, being creatures of intuition. However, because of the artistic sensibilities they exhibit, slothfulness repels them violently.

Almost universally the undines are depicted as female and attractive. We get a brief peek at male undines in the Celtic tradition, living among reeds or river banks. In later history, they moved to marshes, lily pads and damp outgrowths of moss. Here, they fastidiously worked with the liquids in plants, animals and human beings.

In Sioux mythology the water devas had two categories, those of the streams and those of waters below ground. The former look like men, the latter like women. Together they create a many-headed monster that supports the earth.

Another name for the water devas is mermaid or merman. These creatures have numerous mentions in a far broader variety of folklore than I imagined. Those off the coast of Brittany are considered beautiful and sirenlike, gathering the souls of those who die at sea. In Livonia, people believe these are Pharaoh's children who drowned in the Red Sea. In either case, however, these stories seem to indicate a less positive connotation for the devic entities than that of the undine.

In working with Water devas, once one has been contacted and agrees to assist you, fitting behests include:

- helping smooth a relationship with waves of peace and understanding
- improving cash flow or liquidity
- aiding personal ability for social "circulation"
- steadying mind, body or soul, as if floating on gentle waters
- an outpouring of healthful energy
- bringing rain to a needful area
- encouraging an outpouring of intuition, creativity, and the muse (especially when you're experiencing blockage)
- cleansing and mending the heart chakra, the emotional center
- washing away lingering negativity in an area
- transporting messages of support, hope and love to those in need
- figuratively watering a relationship or situation so that it becomes fertile and blossoms into fullness

Note that all these requests are suited to the Water deva's personality, which is based heavily in emotions and a devotion to true beauty.

Water Spirits

Spirits are very unpredictable, and frequently fickle, which means one should always take precautions when requesting their aid. Set up a properly protected Sacred Space, and know to whom or what you're directing your request. Have something nearby to help draw that spirit's energy into your circle even as you did for the deva (see also Elemental Attunement, this chapter and Working Atmosphere and Contacting Devas - Chapter 2). Once the entity arrives, be similarly expedient, polite and wary. Finally, after you dismiss the entity, be sure to close the spiritual entryway through which the being entered. This helps keep your sacred space secure and psychically clean.

Aegir: Teutonic giant whose home was in the sea's depths. Suitable propitiations include a gold coin, beer or wine.

Aganippe: Greek nymph whose waters inspire any who drink of them. Welcome her into the sacred space with poetry.

Apo: Persian personification of water spirits. Call on this spirit in any region where sunlight or moonlight reflects off the water's surface.

Apsares: Hindus believe these are the spirits of brave warriors who have returned to this existence as beautiful water nymphs, haunting rivers and pools. Honor them with song and dance.

Arethusa: Greek nymph of springs and fountains.

Cassotis: Greek nymph of prophetic springs. Both she and Arethusa may be given offerings of spring water.

Coventina: British water nymph goddess who received tribute at a sacred well. Appropriate gifts for Coventina include a coin, feather or a water-born leaf.

Daiera: The Greek daughter of Oceanus whose name means "wise one of the sea."

Gahongan: Iroquois water dwelling spirits. Suitable gifts include plain water or water-worn rocks.

Glaisrig: A Scottish undine who cares for young children and the elderly.

Haurvatat: Persian immortal who rules the waters. Honor Haurvatat with something you regard as your best effort, as this is an immortal whose name means "perfection."

Ice Saints: During April and May, **Mamertius** and **Pancras** were invoked during the middle ages to banish the spirit of winter.

Juturna: Romany nymph of healing springs and wells, specifically associated with the sacred spring near the temple of Vesta. Her festival dates included January 11th and August 23rd as a protectress against fire. Two suitable emblems for Juturna are a horse or a pool of water.

Johul: Teutonic giantess of the glacier, whose siblings include **Frosti** (cold), **Snoer** (snow) and **Drifta** (snow drift). Ice cubes, or shaved ice in the sacred space is a nice touch.

Kelpier: Scottish water spirit that inhabits every lake and stream, and is somewhat malevolent.

Liban: An Irish mermaid. Liban is most easily contacted in one's dream time.

Liwa: Suma Indians of Nicaragua and Honduras consider this an evil water dwelling spirit who possesses his own underwater ship.

Metsulah: Hebrew name for the personification of the sea's depths where wonders dwell. Decorate the sacred space with any items gathered from salt-water environments.

Mudjekeewis: Native American Spirit keeper who presides over the western realms.

Nakki: Finnish water genie that can be propitiated with a coin.

Nereids, the: Greek sea nymphs who help sailors. The sacred number for these entities is 50.

Nimue: Arthurian name for the Lady of the Lake, sometimes also considered a goddess form.

Nix: Teutonic water beings that inhabit freshwater, especially very beautiful regions. They are shapeshifters and have the power of invisibility, with some characteristics similar to mermaids physically. These spirits are considered generally malevolent, although they will sometimes mate with humans.

Nootaikok: Eskimo ice spirit. Honor him with an ice carving of a seal.

Rain Saints: Medard and **Barnabas** are the most popular, the first making rain, the second chasing it away.

Thiassi: Teutonic ice giant whose daughter, **Skadi** personified winter, and whose brother, **Thrym** was the frost. Another spirit to whom ice cubes or shaved ice is an appropriate gift.

Tootega: An Eskimo spirit that can walk on water. Bring water-worn stones or ice into the sacred space.

Tonx: Finno-Ugric spirit who overcomes sickness and disease.

Varuna & Anjana: Hindu guardian spirit of the west and its protective elephant who supports that quarter of creation, respectively. Elephant carvings or images of the world are excellent decorations in your Sacred Space for this Being.

Vestri: Norse dwarf of the west who rules water.

Vila: Slavonic water spirit known for graciousness. Have young children, pets or other youthful images in your Sacred Space.

Vu-Kutis: Finno-Ugric disease-curing water spirit.

Vu-Nuna: Finno-Ugric water spirit and defender.

Wave Maidens, the: Teutonic giantesses who mothered **Heimdall**, the great Aesir and god of light. Welcome the Wave Maidens with a candle whose light reflects off a bowl or glass of water.

Water Deities

When working with the Water element, it is sometimes useful to call on a specific divine persona, associated with Water, to empower your efforts. In so doing, one should always acquaint themselves with that persona before hand by learning what that God/dess holds sacred, and how to pronounce their name correctly (among other things). Set up your sacred space so it honors that power, and call upon it with respectful humility.

The information below provides only a brief overview of the gods and goddesses associated with the element of Water. Beyond this cursory list, any divine entity affiliated with the moon, fertility, healing, and other "watery" characteristics can be an alternative to consider. For more information on Deities of the world, look to texts like The Witches God and The Witches Goddess by Janet and Stewart Farrar, and Bullfinch's Mythology (see also resources).

Adsullata: Celtic goddess of springs. Appease with hot water, or fire and water in the sacred space.

Aleyn: Phoenician god of rain. Crops and other vegetation are suitable offerings.

Alphaeus: Greek river god.

Anahita: Persian sea-goddess, known also as the "golden mother." For best results, call upon her on the 10th day of the New Moon.

Apa: Hindu divine being who personifies water and attends Indra.

Apsu: Assyro-Babylonian sweet water god.

Babi: Egyptian god invoked for protection on rough waters. Bamboo images are sacred to him.

Bacabs, the: Mayan rain and fertility gods. Holy number: 4.

Bannik: Slavonic god of the bathhouse.

Bau: Assyro-Babylonian goddess of deep water and health. Bring harvest items to your alter to honor her.

Beltis: Assyro-Babylonian goddess of wells and springs. Decorate the circle with fallen tree twigs.

Cerridwen: Welsh moon goddess whose caldron held the liquid of wisdom and inspiration. Sacred items appropriate for your alter include pieces of chicken or pork, or corn.

Chalchiuhtlicue: Aztec goddess of running water.

Ciaga: Nicaraguan creative water god.

Copacati: Incan goddess of lakes. Honor her with having a bowl with a submerged castle, like those available at fish shops.

Daiera: Greek "wise woman of the sea."

Demeter: Greek goddess who had a divinatory well that foretold the outcome of a sickness. Leave sunflower seeds on your altar and burn myrrh. Celebratory dates include 9/23, 10/1, 10/4, 10/13 and 12/22.

Dylan: Welsh sea god who married the Lady of the Lake. Give him an offering of fish.

Ea: Babylonian/Chaldaean water god whose name means "house of water." Also the god of wisdom, learning, magic, divination and knowledge.

Egeria: Roman oracular water goddess. Call on this goddess during evening hours.

Gasmu: Chaldaean goddess of the sea and wisdom. Leave seeds on your altar for her.

Hler: Scandinavian god of the sea, as the stiller of storms.

Juturna: Roman goddess of lakes and streams. Festival dates include 1/11 and 8/23.

Kawa-no-Kami: Japanese general term for a river god.

Latis: British goddess whose tears are the winter rains. Suitable offerings include beer and salmon.

Mama Cocha: Incan female deity whose domains are the sea and rain. As a libation, mix equal portions of milk with water.

Manannan: Irish sea god whose visage may have been based on an adept ailing merchant. Even into the early 1900s fishermen could be heard calling on this divinity to bless their boats and catches. Bring a cauldron or fishing net into the magic circle to honor him.

Mara: Chaldaean salt-sea mother. Use salt water as a libation.

Mari: A Celtic sea goddess to whom all water creatures are sacred. Decorate the circle with red hues, wool or broomsticks.

Matsyavatra: The first incarnation of Vishnu, half man-half fish, who saved humankind from the deluge.

Mirmir: Scandinavian god of the ocean or open sea who lives in the roots of the Yggdrasil from which he drinks to know all things. Burn bits of ashwood to him when stating your desires.

Mithras: In pre-Zoroastrian Persia, this god regulated the water's circulation, even though he is commonly considered "solar" in nature. Consequently, keep yellow and gold as predominant colors to the sacred space.

Mitshua-nome-no-kami: Japanese water goddess.

Nakki: Finnish water god. Call on this deity at sunrise or sunset.

Nanshe: Assyro-Babylonian goddess of springs and canals whose holy symbol was a fish in a crystal vase (like our modern goldfish bowl).

Neith: Egyptian goddess whose domain was the waters of chaos and creation. Woven items and bows & arrows are sacred to her. Neith's festival day is June 24.

Nereus: Greek. The "old man of the sea." The most precious gift you can give this Being is the truth!

Ningirsu: Assyro-Babylonian god of irrigation. Call your wishes into a southerly wind so Ningirsu hears them.

Niord: Scandinavian god of coastal waters, fishing, commerce and prosperity.

Nu: Egyptian god who presided over the world-ocean. Appropriate decorations for the circle include frogs, topaz, aspen branches, fans and daggers.

Oannes: Babylonian fish-tailed god who gave humankind culture.

Oceanus: Early Greek god who forms a liquid circuit around the universe, and from whom all waters originated.

Parjanya: Vedic god of the rain, and the personification of rain clouds;also a fertility god. Also has solar overtones, so yellow is a good color to highlight your circle.

Pontus: Early Greek god who personified the ocean.

Poseidon: The Greek god of the sea. Equated with Neptune in Rome. Burn cedar incense and have amethyst on your altar to welcome his presence.

Rutbe: Costa Rican water goddess.

Shiu-mu Niang-Niang: Chinese water mother. Sacred symbols include lanterns and dragons.

Shoney: Irish & Scottish sea god, especially for fishermen. Traditionally, Shoney is offered ale.

Tefnut: Egyptian goddess of dew and rain. Honor her with tears or lion images.

Tiamat: Assyro-Babylonian primordial sea goddess. Tiamat's animals are the dragon or serpent.

Untunktahe: Dakota god of water and magical mastery.

Varuna: Vedic water god who maintains justice and order. Offer him a libation of spirits.

Vellamo: Finnish sea goddess who also rules all earthly waters. The name comes from a word that means "to rock oneself" as the waves do.

Whale Goddess: Arabic tradition has it that the world rests on the back of this creature and earthquakes are the result of its shaking tail.

Correspondence List

ANIMALS & INSECTS: All water-dwelling creatures and amphibians. Alligator, beaver, black bear (Native American), crab, crane, crocodile, dolphin, duck, frog, kingfisher, loon, otter, pelican, penguin, porpoise, seagull, seal, sea lions, silver dragon (China), snow leopard (also earth), swan, toads, turtle, walrus, water snakes. Also the fabled water horse of Welsh and English folklore, called *ceffyl dwr* and *shoopiltee*, respectively.

APPLICATIONS: Beauty, cleansing, creativity, dreams, friendship, fertility, forgiveness, health & healing, intuition, emotions, gentle love, maternal feelings, moon magic, movement, patience, peace, psychic, the subconscious self, and spiritual awareness.

ARCHANGEL: Gabriel or Raphael.

ASTROLOGICAL SIGNS: Pisces, Cancer, Scorpio; also Aquarius while not a traditional water sign, this is the water bearer.

CELESTIAL INFLUENCES: The moon.

COLORS: Grey (Celtic); Green (Enochian, Mexican); Black (Mayan, Native American); White or silver (China, Cheyenne); Yellow (Navaho); Blue (Zuni).

CRYSTALS, MINERALS, STONES: Amethyst, aquamarine, blue lace agate, azurite, beryl, copper, coral, emerald, holey stones, jade, lapis, lodestone, mercury (quicksilver), moonstone, mother-of-pearl, pink calcite, quartz, sapphire, seashells, silver, sodalite, sugilite, tourmaline (blue or green).

DIRECTION: Traditionally West. East (Mexico). Note, however, if a body of water lies in another direction near your home, you may wish to consider honoring this element in that quadrant instead.

Consider some type of ritual cleansing before embarking on your rite.

EMBLEMS: Beach ball, cauldron, cups, driftwood, feathers from seabirds (like gulls), fog, holey stones, horns, icicle, kelp fronds, mist, mermaid, moon, rain, sand, sea salt, sea horse (or images of other sea creatures), seashells, snow, steam, a wave, any container holding liquid (especially water).

FOOD ITEMS (MISC): Bagel, beechnuts, beverages (most), carob, coconut, hazelnut, ice cream, licorice, milk, poppy seed, soup, spirulina, sugar cane, yogurt. Most seafood and steam-cooked items.

FRUITS & VEGETABLES: Apple, apricot, avocado, banana, berries, broccoli, brussel sprouts, cabbage, cauliflower, cherry, coconut, cranberry (also Fire), cucumber, grape, grapefruit, guava, lemon, lentil, lettuce, melon, nectarine, papaya, passion fruit, pea, peach, pear, persimmon, plum, sweet potato (also Earth), tomato, watermelon.

GENDER: Feminine.

GREEK SHAPE: Icosahedral.

HEBRAIC QUARTER: Achor or "behind."

HERBS: Camphor, caper, cardamom, catnip, chamomile, chickweed, comfrey, eucalyptus, licorice, myrrh, orris, spearmint, thyme, vanilla, wintergreen.

MOON PHASE: Waxing.

MOONS (Folk Names): Ice Moon (January), Storm Moon (February), Fish Moon (March), Frog Moon (April), Milking Moon and Hare Moon (May), Rain Moon and Whale Moon (July), Moon of Spawning Salmon (August), Wine Moon (October), Snow Moon (November) Little Manitou Moon (December).

PLACES: Creeks, dewy surfaces, faucets, fountains, geysers, lake fronts, ponds, puddles, rain forest, rain spouts, river banks, sea shore, springs, sprinklers, waterfalls, waterspouts, wells.

PLANTS, TREES, & FLOWERS: Alder, aloe, ash, aster, beech, birch, buckthorn, crocus, daffodil, daisy, elder, elm, fern, foxglove, gardenia, hazel, hemlock, heather, iris, jasmine, kelp, lilac, lily, lotus, mesquite, morning glory, moss, orchid, pansy, poplar, poppy, rose, rushes, sandalwood, violet, willow, all water-dwelling plants.

SEASON: Autumn, or the traditionally rainy season of a region. Also late winter, due to thawing snows.

SENSE: Taste.

TATTWAS SYMBOL (INDIA): Apas—a silver crescent turned upward.

TAROT EMBLEMS: Cups, shells, bowls, cauldrons. The Moon Card for its influence, and the Empress for her creative force.

TIME: Twilight.

WIND (Name): Zephyrus (the west wind).

"Water" by Colleen Koziara

"Earth" by Colleen Koziara

Gaia is weeping
as her tears pour forth
all that dwells above and below drinks
of one common cup;
the soil, the rivers, the oceans
these are the grail.

See her in beauty:
lush green hair flowing, across the plains
a curved body, earth pregnant with potential
windy breath, scented by flowers
eyes at each pole, searching the universe
bowers embracing the light of the stars.

Truly this is Mother
a font of life
foundations that nurture the questing spirit
sacred loam that enriches the soul

Give to Her the seed of self
to grow
into wholeness

Chapter Four
Earth

"From house to house he goes, sure and slight, be there rain or snow, he sleeps outside all night.
— Old Riddle whose answer is "an earthen path."

While our places of birth are many, the home for all humankind is the earth. The constituents of this special planet provided all the building blocks necessary that life might form. When that miracle finally happened, the second home it found was on *terra firma*—land.

As the first creatures crawled from the oceans, one must wonder what spectacular sights awaited them. Nature was unbridled, growing furiously, vividly and abundantly. When humankind finally found their footing in this ancient, wild world, they could not have been unaffected by the enormity of it all.

Our earliest progenitors made their homes in caves, the

womb of the earth. It was in this protective sphere that communities developed, as did we. Yet, humans could not always stay in that cave. They had to venture out, explore, hunt, and gather, and as they did earth's beauties did not go unnoticed. A delicate flower may have been tried for food, or a beautiful leaf taken back home as a gift.

Later, when greater powers of reasoning developed, humans began to worship the earth and each living thing as having a spirit. While this animistic outlook has long since waned, the spirit known as Earth still affects us deeply, as does her body. Consequently, the Earth element is very important to understanding who we are as a people, where we have come from and where we are going together.

The Earth is an element that touches all other elements. It cannot be separated from them. Air is the breath of Gaia, the fire (sun) and water provide nourishment, and Spirit gave Earth life. In touching a handful of soil, one may touch the whole earth, its history, and all other elements consecutively.

Just as one cannot separate Earth from the other elements, we cannot discuss this element without likewise touching on nature. Victorian writers and artists reminded us again that nature's bounty reflects the intricate simplicity of universal law and divine lessons. For example, stones teach the lesson of patience and reflect the aphorism of "all things in their time," and seeds patiently await birth in the soil, even as some cultures believe the soul to do.

The Earth element has strong associations with foundation and solidarity, yet it is also a growing force that protects and nurtures the soul. Biblically, soil is of what humankind was made, and the land was humankind's first source of sustenance and protection. This makes earth both literally and figuratively our mother. Consequently, this mother teaches our soul in her classroom (this planet) so we can integrate past lessons, and blossom toward enlightenment. Nearly all sages have recognized this intimate connection, and therefore have honored the earth in the way they lived. This may also explain the prevalence of Earth worship around the word.

Myths And Legends

People as far removed as the Zuni Indians, Peruvians and Native Americans have all regarded the Earth as a Mother figure, having the same life-giving power as a fertile woman. Consequently it is not surprising to discover Native American myths discussing the soul as waiting for rebirth under the ground in earth's womb. Similarly, in Christian tradition clay was likened to human flesh. These correlations may indicate why the funerary tradition of burial began, relinquishing the body back to the earth for renewal.

The themes of humankind being produced from soil or clay, or appearing from an underground waiting area with the aid of an outside force (Spirit), repeat themselves in several settings. In Greek mythology, Prometheus formed humankind from earth and water. In Sumeria, Ninmah fashioned people from clay. And, in Guatemala, god made men first from mud but they could not stand, then from wood but they were self centered, and finally from clay which could be carefully carved into a likeness of the Divine. Bearing this last story in mind, and that of Genesis, it is not surprising that nearly every culture represents god similarly to themselves. After all, don't children often look like their parents?

In Greek mythology we find Gaea, the personification of Earth. This goddess presides over the land and all it produces. She is also a fertility figure. In this tradition, Gaea was born from chaos and then she gave birth to the heavens and the sea. Gaea was also connected with the underworld and rebirth. Consequently, the Oracle at Delphi, famed to reside in the Earth's navel, first belonged to her. In Roman tradition this goddess translated into Tellus or Terra.

The Earth is an element that touches all other elements.

Among the Egyptians, four different deities try to take credit for the Earth's creation; Ptah, Osiris, Thothe and Ra. Each creation myth, however, is slightly different. One god creates with the word, another with sweat or tears, and another yet with mud from the Nile. It is interesting to note that despite these claims, it is Geb who is depicted in Egyptian art as the earth, neatly sprouting vegetation on his back. Geb's twin sister is Nut, the sky.

As a moving sphere, the Kato Indians (CA) tell of the earth as being a horned creature that moves eternally through the waters of creation. North American tribes often refer to the Earth as an island floating in water, presumably the sea of space. Beyond this many creation myths discuss an animal who dives into primeval or flood waters to retrieve the first loam of what would becomes land.

The Seneca Indians, for example, talk of the oeh-da, the bit of dirt brought up from the sea by Muskrat. This earth was considered great enough for the blinding light of Ataensic to rest upon as she descended from the sky (e.g. the sun). The Turtle offered to hold the oeh-da as it grew, becoming a large island. To this day, legend has it that when Turtle is tired and moves a little, the earthquakes and tidal waves come. This type of story, and others like it, creates a very powerful link between the earth element and that of water — water being able to both create and destroy the land.

Various types of occurrences on the planet also have interesting mythological origins. In the Far East people believe that earthquakes are caused by a dragon's jumping up and down. In Timor, this occurs when a giant shifts his hold on the earth from one shoulder to another. The Burmese believe a great fish sleeps beneath the planet with its tail in its mouth. When it wakens and bites the tail, the surprise causes upheaval. Finally, my favorite explanation occurs among Africans where an earthquake represents god's voice to which one should immediately reply.

Eco-spirituality's Affect On Earth devas

Eco-spirituality is very important to our overall study of the devas, especially the earth devas, since they are part of the planet's matrix. This importance is something that our forebears knew well, warning that one should never selfishly misuse nature spirits (specifically, the gnomes). The implied risk went far beyond harm to the magus, but to harming the web of life itself.

So, our notions of eco-spirituality are actually based on far older ideas, stemming at least in part from earth worship. The standing stones throughout Europe are but one timeless reminder of our ancestors' veneration of earth and its powers.

From Greek philosophers musing that trees have souls, to Saints who viewed nature as god's visual teacher, early people were avid naturalists, albeit often unwittingly.

In terms of the modern eco-spirituality movement, other sources of inspiration are most easily traced to the Victorian Era when the post-Raphaelite artists and writers praised nature and the earth with every stroke and point. Another upsurge in our focus on the earth came during the 1980s when the United Nations created a World Charter for Nature. This charter offered a guideline that would help protect the planet's environment.

The outlook that regards the earth as sacred, and not just a toy for our pleasure, is one necessary to properly motivated elemental study and successful devic contact. We cannot expect *any* deva to honor our requests if we don't likewise honor the thing that gives and sustains their life; the earth. This also means that the Earth elementals are incredibly important to global healing at this juncture in history. Their task is a large one that we can help in small ways, one of which is by not calling them away from their work unless the need is urgent (or perhaps global in nature). Please bear this in mind, while developing a growing Gaian awareness, as you work with the earth element.

Folklore, Superstition, Magick

As one might expect, the lore of the Earth element is far different from that of water. The thematic goals of using earth (or other of nature's symbols) often mirror, at least in part, those of the other elements, but the processes change to suit that element's character.

Divination

• In Russia, people dig in the earth then place their ear to the hole to listen to earth's voice. They believe if you know the earth's language, it can answer questions with regard to the future. If, for example, they hear the sound of an empty sleigh going over the land, it is a bad omen for crops that year.

• Scottish girls used to dig a hole in the dirt at the intersection of three roads then place their ear to it to hear the voice of a future lover. Similarly, in England people dug a hole in the 3rd and 4th furrow of a field and listened to hear their future lover's trade sounds.

• In the Far East handfuls of dust are tossed in the air, and the resulting patterns are interpreted for omens and signs. This is a type of Geomancy.

Fertile Soil/Farming

• One should not dig in the earth on Good Friday as this causes barren fields.

• To insure that you will have a good harvest, offer the earth gifts of bread, cheese, wine and ale when you first prepare the soil.

• Bury a jar with twelve crayfish and river water in the soil near your garden. This safeguards the crops from a late frost.

• Moss agates and moonstones buried in the soil of a garden or field will improve yield and health of all that grows thereon.

Health

• To prevent disease, gather three handfuls of earth from a molehill thrice and mix them with vinegar. Replace in the molehill.

• Spit in a hole in the earth, or in a tree trunk to transfer disease from yourself to the earth. Cover the hole afterwards. Alternatively, bury a sage leaf with the name of the malady on it. The sickness will wane with the leaf.

• Plant a tree on the birth of a child, and the child will grow as strong and sure as the tree.

• Soil gathered from sacred ground cures illness, specially that taken from a graveyard. In Ireland this is mixed with water to effect wellness by way of symbolically overcoming death.

• Placing healthful herbs in the soil from an ailing person's footprint will speed their recovery.

• Write the name of the malady on elder wood and place it in damp soil to rot away. As the wood wanes, so will the sickness.

• To cure a fever, take salt to a cross road once a day at sunset. Do this for five days and the fever will be gone.

Hunting

• Before an important hunt, African tribal members put charms in the soil to draw the appropriate creatures to them self.

Love

• Carrying soil or sand from a person's foot prints in a red flannel bag compels them to stay close to you and be faithful.

• Plant acorns with the name of the one you love in rich soil so that love continues to grow.

• To keep a lover true, take earth from their footsteps along with a strand of your hair and mix this with wine. Drink and it will keep that person ever close to you.

• To deter the affections of an unwanted suitor, write an X on a sage leaf and bury it in the soil near the suitor's home. When the leaf falls apart, they will lose interest in you.

Luck

• If you find a black feather, stick it upright in fertile soil to encourage good fortune.

• To keep luck, money, love and family in the home, always sweep the dust in your home toward the center and gather it there. To sweep it out the door, sweeps away fortune.

Oath Taking

• Slaves swear their oaths on earth, asking it to bear witness on any land or property agreements. Once the earth has heard the pledge it is binding and uncontestible.

• In Arabia, it is not uncommon to take an oath with salt to keep the oath pure.

• When any agreements were made over land, it was often the custom to exchange a handful of the dirt from that land with the deed as a binding tie.

Protection

• Russians dug holes in the earth just prior to difficult battles so its spirit could fight for them. The opening in the ground releases this spirit for the duration of need.

• If you feel someone is trying to inflict harm on you, erase the outline made by their foot in the dirt. This likewise erases negativity.

• Bury an object in rich soil by the light of a full moon to exorcise a negative spell cast upon it. Leave it there until the next full moon. Sometimes the waning moon is used for this action, because of the shrinking size (e.g. to decrease power).

• Throwing a handful of earth at fairies on Hallows Eve will force them to avert any mischief on you, and they will also give back any human beings they are keeping among them.

• Placing bones or sharp objects in the soil or mud from a person's footprints will turn back any negative energy they've directed your way.

Prosperity

• At twilight, sweep bits of dirt near your home toward the door. The Scots believe this draws in prosperity.

• When cleaning your home on New Year's, be certain to gather all dust to the center of the house to keep wealth likewise centered there.

• Bury a gold or silver coin in the light of a waxing to full moon so money can grow.

Wishes

• Among some tribal cultures such as the Menkiera, people offer sacrifices to rocks and stones in order to help fulfill desires, especially for a region over which these spirits can exert their powers.

Earth Attunement

Just as before with Water, the best way to get to know this element is through direct contact with Earth in many forms. An idea along this line might be to spend more time doing indoor or outdoor gardening, allowing the soil to seep through your fingers as you work. Or, try a mud bath or beauty pack some day when you want a little pampering.

Additionally, go to regions that exhibit earth in different forms. If more than one form can be found at the same sight, terrific! This gives you a chance to compare directly. Find a rocky terrain, a sandy area, a field where the earth is rich and damp, and another tract that is barren. Make notes of how each area feels and smells in your journal. If you cannot find a rocky or sandy terrain, use a bowl full of sand from an aquarium or children's toy store, and/or a dish filled with small tumbled stones instead. Both will give you the same textural input as the outdoor environment.

While you might not think the Earth has a voice as clear as that of water and its waves, one does exist. People often describe it sounding like a low, rich thrum or throb, akin to a heartbeat only coming from deep within the planet. It is this sound, some speculate, that lead to the development of drums as a musical expression, trying to capture that earthly sound. It does take longer to develop a knack for hearing Earth, and this must be

According to the Bible, humankind had its genesis in the soil.

done in a quiet remote location where other noise pollution won't hinder your efforts. Nonetheless the time is very well spent. Once you know earth's voice, you also know the voice of nature and of our world. From here it is much easier to discern how best to use Earth's lessons, and heed its needs.

Earth teaches us much, especially that growth in our lives means that we must change. Every season, every plant that starts at seed and returns to seed, every creature that begins small and grows to fullness reminds us of this truth. If something cannot grow, it stagnates and eventually dies; this includes our spirit.

Earth also teach us that foundations are important, but even the best foundations are not without weaknesses. The mighty oak can be taken down by the hand of nature's fury as easily as one might snap a toothpick. This means that we cannot build our spirituality upward without first sinking our roots down toward the Mother, and holding firm to Her truths.

The Earth is also a gentle nurturing element, exhibiting the lesson of patience and all things in their time. The seed's growth cannot be rushed or forced. A baby animal cannot be born too soon without increased potential dangers. So too, our spiritual growth must have a pace that allows for steady integration of lessons, and continued stretching toward the Light.

Earth Healing

According to the Bible, humankind had its genesis in the soil. This is not an ideal limited to Judeo-Christian beliefs, however. Certain tribal cultures, including the Indians of North America, believe that the soul waits for rebirth underground, and that the earth is the beginning and end of all life. With this in mind, soil takes on a cultivational, sustaining characteristic, easily applied symbolically to healing.

For example, the holistic therapy known as bodywork increases a patient's awareness of their elemental self. Chiropractics and osteopaths specifically try to manipulate the body and retrain the individual to live in better harmony with earth, especially gravity. In earlier times, folk healers often buried people in the earth to create a mock death so the spirit of sickness would be fooled into leaving. While these two worlds seem light-years apart in approach, the underlying theme is the same. The Earth has the power to help make us well.

Here are a few illustrations that you can try yourself. None are overly difficult, and require little else than a respectful attitude on the part of the participants. If you wish to accent your efforts astrologically, wait to try these when the moon is in Taurus, Virgo or Capricorn, or use the seasons as an additional guide. For example, working on emotional healing for a long-lived anger might be best accomplished in Fall or Winter, a time of cooling.

Clay: Terrific for facials, easing the itch of insect bites and other skin toning. For most effectiveness, the clay should be free of small stones and other debris, and should be applied warm.

Dust: Gather dust from beneath a stone at a crossroads. Rub the effected part of your body with it, then throw it away to the left of you. Alternatively, gather dust from a grave site (please don't desecrate Holy Ground in the process) and carry this with you as a health and longevity charm. Symbolically this provides victory over death.

Herbs: Choose symbolic herbs for banishing (like garlic) and wrap them in a person-shaped cloth made from a piece of clothing that you've warn. Burn or bury this to destroy the malady.

Holey Stones: People of Cornwall, England pass themselves through the Menantol as a symbolic passage from sickness to health. Since this may not be feasible for most folks, try carrying a stone with a natural hole in it instead as a healthful amulet.

Lodestone: This gets laid on, or carried near, the area of dis-ease or sickness to figuratively "draw out" any lingering negative energy. Afterwards the lodestone should be buried far away from people so the negativity can naturally flow out to the earth.

Rocks: In Africa, specially painted rocks often get placed outside of homes or whole villages to keep the spirit of disease away. For your personal version of such a stone, I suggest choosing personally meaningful sigils (like runes), paint them on by hand a symbolic number of times, then set the stone where you want it during a waning moon for banishing, or a waxing moon to draw positive, protective energies.

Salt: Salt has a natural cleansing and protective quality. It is an excellent addition to healing baths and amulets, and in some cases works very well to combat infection. For example, for gum problems rinse your mouth twice daily with salt water.

Sand: Go to a beach someday when everything aches and let a child bury you in the warm, golden grains. I guarantee its fun for the child, and you'll feel better after about 20 minutes. Take care to wear proper sunscreen on your face.

Alternatively, Native Americans use sand painting as a ritual form of healing. For the sand painting to be effective, the patient should sit in the middle. Work begins in the elemental colors of white, blue, yellow, black and red around them. The sacred image should be created and destroyed in the span of a day while prayers and songs are recited. Afterward, the sand is given to the wind to carry sickness away.

Soil: Instead of burying yourself in soil, carry a token with you for 7 or 12 days visualizing your malady flowing into it. Then, bury this token in the soil to bury the sickness. Above it, place a flowering seed so something good can come from your experience. Figuratively, you are giving the Mother your "dirt," which She knows how to deal with quite well!

Earth Meditation & Visualization

For people who have trouble keeping one foot on the ground, or those who find the smallest troubles seem to knock them off kilter, earth meditations are an ideal aid. Earth not only provides the foundations you may not have developed, but also nurtures those foundations.

Begin by sitting in an upright position with your back against a wall. Close your eyes and breath deeply, allowing your tensions and worries to fade away until nothing exists but you, the beating of your heart and your breath. As this calmness settles, begin visualizing yourself as you are now, only outside in the midst of a beautiful forest, brimming with life.

When the forest becomes clear, focus your attention on your legs and feet which touch the earth below you. Slowly they transform, growing little shoots that reach for the soil. These new roots grow larger, and bark begins to form around them to protect their connection to Gaia. As the roots develop, your waist and torso also become bark-like, now appearing much like the trunk of a tree. Feel how firm and strong you are, how your roots enjoy the earth's cool nectars.

Finally, your arms and head begin to experience the metamorphosis. They become branches and leaves that reach ever upward as if to hold the sun close. Now step back and look at the tree of self. It is well grounded in the Mother-soil, yet has aspirations that touch the sky. This is the gift of earth; it provides a sound basis from which dreams can grow into realities.

An alternative visualization to help connect you more strongly with the planet and the earth element begins similarly. This time, however, imagine that the forest in which you sit is near the opening of a cavern. Stand in your visualization (and physically if it helps) and stretch, then begin making your way to the cavern.

Once inside, the darkness surrounds you, but it is not

frightening. Instead it is like the comforting darkness that comes just before sleep; fertile, rich and welcoming. As you continue to walk, your feet lead you ever downward further and further into earth's womb. Here, you can hear the ebb and flow of Gaia herself. It is a subtle music, similar to the song of your heart's beating.

Sit in this sacred place and commune with that sound as long as you wish. You may sense small, stout figures near you from time to time. Don't be concerned, these are just the gnomes "checking you out." If the darkness distracts you, allow a pale luminescence to resonate from the cavern walls. Change the color of this light to mirror any specific personal goals for your visualization, for example:

Red: Increasing physical energy.

Orange: The abundance that comes from harvesting the results of your hard labors, and well tended plans.

Yellow/Gold: Flourishing potential for incomes.

Green: Successful growth or maturity in any area of your life.

Blue: Peace at your work place, or peaceful resolution to a legal matter.

Purple: Spiritual understanding of the cycles in your life, and their purpose or lessons.

As before, continue with your visualization until you feel you've accomplished as much as possible within that time. Note your experiences.

Rituals

In devising Earth rituals, there are two approaches to be considered. First are those rituals which honor and extend energy to the planet Earth. Second are those rituals in which the element of Earth is honored and used as a vehicle for magic. I feel it important to discuss both herein.

As mentioned earlier this chapter, earth healing and awareness is very important to our work with the devas. As the planet gets injured, the associated devic energies are also injured or forced away. So rituals that extend magic to the planet like a salve, also aid our elemental allies.

Potential dates for Earth-healing rites follow in the Holiday Observances section of this chapter. Exactly what you do during those gatherings is as limitless as your imagination and elbow grease will allow. I do, however, suggest combining metaphysical efforts with concrete actions for best results. Begin with a prayer or meditation for the planet, with visualizations of the earth being wrapped in a healthy green light that acts like a bandage to the world's wounds. Afterwards have recycling collections, garbage pick ups, educational classes etc. so that the body of earth is also served.

In the realms of the traditional magic circle, the Earth element is often represented with a pentagram set up in the Northern quarter of the sacred space. During spring rituals and land blessings, a group's leader will frequently provide rich soil to distribute among all members. This symbolically allows them to transport home the fertile energies generated during ritual to their land, gardens and window boxes.

For rituals centering their focus on any theme appropriate to Earth, rich soil can mark the line between the worlds. One example might be a blessing way where the child is touched to the soil to reveal another important Mother figure in their lives. Additionally, salt as an earth component is a good marker for the outer circle, having a strong protective and purgative nature.

Spellcraft

The Earth element, above all others, offers us a diversity of applications in spellcraft. From soil and sand to the entire component pantry of nature herself, there are very few spells that don't integrate this element in some way. Some examples for your consideration include:

Dirt: Have you ever heard the saying "walking in someone else's shoes?" In folk tales there are numerous examples of footprints that bring transformation just by stepping into them. For spellcraft, this might equate to choosing a shoe that represents your goal, like picking a sneaker if you desire a position on a sport's team. Then during your spell's casting, literally put that shoe on to don the magic!

Another application for dirt is, believe it or not, in cleansing spells. Dust yourself with a little dust or dirt so that you have a physical, visible reality to wash off during your spellcraft. This sensual input improves the success of your working.

Herbs & Plant Matter: Nearly every part of nature has been used at some juncture in history for spells. In some cases the herbs or plants became potions, in others incense, in others yet they were physical components whose transformation mirrored the goal of the magic. For example, tossing rose petals on the ground leading to your home is one way of welcoming love therein.

Pebbles: I like charging pebbles with the magic generated by a spell and carrying them, or scattering them around the area where that energy is needed most. Additionally, larger stones make excellent elemental markers for the sacred space.

Salt: In spells, salt is best used as a purifying component, as the phrase "salt of the earth" has come to imply. When you feel your intentions or those of others need improvement, or when you wish to banish negative energies or spirits from a region or object, try salt in your spellcraft's equation.

Sand: Thanks to the nursery stories of western Europe regarding the Sand Man, this type of earth is a perfect component for sleep, rest and sanctuary magic.

Soil: After particularly intense rituals or spells, one may need to "ground" excess energy to return to normal levels of awareness. The easiest way to accomplish this is by sitting on a patch of soil, putting your fingertips into it, and allowing the energies to seep out of you.

To root energy to a specific location, plant an object that

represents your spell in the soil at that location. This acts as a permanent energy beacon, that can be renewed whenever you feel the need. Additionally, the imagery of planting anything in rich soil is very effective for spellcraft, as you anticipate growing energy from such actions.

Holiday Observances

In terms of timing your earth element spells or rituals, here are some festivals and celebrations that may accentuate your goals:

New Year's Day: A traditional time for crop omens and signs. Animals were often given blessed wheat to protect them from sickness and harm in the coming year.

12th Day: In England farmers often blessed their harvest today by dancing around 12 fires in their fields and toasting the apple trees with wassail or cider. Dalmatians sprinkle their farms and animals with holy water to bless them.

1st Monday after 12th Day: This is Plough Monday when farmers return to their fields after the holidays with a joyful heart. A good day to bless seeds or soil.

1st Monday of the New Year: In Scotland this is Handsel Monday when workers and those who serve are often given special monetary gifts to honor their efforts. A good day for prosperity magic.

1/23 New Year of the Trees: Jewish tree-planting festival that is part of the agricultural rejuvenation of Israel. Any type of planting or seeding is appropriate today.

1/24 Ekiko's Fair: The Bolivian god of prosperity and abundance is honored today.

1/27 Roman Planting Festival: This invoked the blessings of Ceres, Prosperina and Tellus.

2/1 St. Brigidt's Day (Candlemas): St. Brigidt is thought by some to have been an Irish fairy who took special interest in, and care of, young children and woodland creatures.

2/6 Chinese New Year: Part of this festival includes a special offering of thanks to the Earth. Also, the first seven days of the New Year observe the birthdays of various animals and plants.

Lent: One of the traditional fasting times, specifically giving up of meat. A nice time to honor earth's creatures by abstaining from meat for a duration of time suitable to your health constraints.

2/23 Terminalia: Roman festival where the land and boundaries were blessed with flowers and prayers.

3/8 Chinese Earth Mother Festival: Rice, sugar dates and beans are left for this goddess to encourage abundance and productive soil.

3/25 Spring Equinox: The festival that honors the rebirth of Earth after winter's chill is broken.

Late April, Early May, Arbor Day or Earth Day: Arbor day is traditionally a tree-planting festival, where Earth day is more modern in origin thanks to the ecological movement.

May Day: A happy celebration of flowers and fertility,

marking the time when everything on the Earth begins to show signs of life through blossoms and greenery.

6/12 Riding the Marches: Scottish festival very similar to terminalia in Roman times.

8/1 Lamas: The beginning of two months of various harvest festivals that rejoice in Earth's bounty and give thanks for same.

8/2 Day of the Dryads: Macedonian festival during which no vine was cut or washing done to remember the spirits of the woods and waters.

9/7 Festival of Durga: Honoring the Hindu goddess who represents the earth's energy. Traditionally, all personal quarrels are also settled during the five day duration of this celebration.

10/4 St. Francis of Assisi Day: This very special man considered the animals and birds his "little brothers and sisters."

11/29 (est) Thanksgiving: Another well known harvest festival where sharing of the Earth's bounty and gifts to you is quite fitting.

12/19 Chinese Winter Solstice: Traditionally people leave offerings in the trees to bring joy to the land.

Working With Earth Devas

Taken from a word meaning knowledge or "earth dweller," gnomes are hard working, happy, tenacious and pragmatic Earth devas, formed from terreous ether. They also have a keen sense of humor when interacting with humans. Chari-

table, jovial, considerate, honest and industrious individuals attract them the most strongly, while those who exhibit deception
or irritability repel them. Generally speaking, gnomes cherish
the earth and love their sense of orderliness. Earth devas, in
order to be functional, must exist in a vibrational plane very
close to that of physical nature. Pygmies work with stones and
gems, often guarding hidden treasure. The Scandinavians believed this particular gnome dwelled in caves below the mythical
Land of Nibelungen.

Tree forest spirits include satyrs, dryads, elves, and others. Some choose to live in groups while others are independent,
remaining indigenous to a specific substance (e.g. a plant, tree,
mineral, etc.). Every plant and stone has a manifesting earth
deva who often looks like their place of residence. Those connected to the mighty oak, for example, would be larger than
other gnomes.

Among the Iroquois, the dwarfish spirits have three categories. First is the Gahongas who live in water and rocks. Second are the Gandayaks who make vegetation grow and care for
the fish of the rivers. Third are Ohdowas who live underground
taking charge over monsters and venomous beasts.

In Scandinavian tradition dwarves are called dvergar.
This creature, if captured, will pay huge ransoms to secure their
freedom. These beings live in the hills and mountains where
they mine treasures.

In New Zealand, dwarves are described generally as
hairy men of wood. In Fiji they appear as having white skin.

Additionally, in these and other oceanic cultures nearly every island, volcano, valley and ravine has a specific spirit or demi-deity with characteristics that one might expect from such locations. For example, the rock elemental might be very slow to communicate and rather dull.

The Brownies and Dwarves (a type of Fey) in European folk tales might also be considered in this category. Like the gnomes, both are very hard working creatures. Brownies enjoy helping humans who show steadfastness, and dwarves are masters of stone working, living deep in the mountainsides where they toil tirelessly to mine various substances. Additionally, if a dwarf, who often appears elderly and grayish in complexion, gives you a small gift, keep it! This will turn to gold in your hand once they leave, and is a sign of favor among the Earth elementals.

Some philosophers theorize that the Earth devas meet periodically through the year to rejoice in Nature and celebrate good harvests. These beings are depicted as wearing clothing made from plants or other natural items, and as having ferocious appetites. Consequently, small gifts of food are an excellent way to tempt Earth devas into visiting, and staying, in a location.

Appropriate behests for Earth devas include:

• Improving your appreciation and understanding of nature's symbols and lessons.

• Helping create solid foundations in which a dream or goal may take root.

• Aiding in matters of emotional, spiritual or physical growth and/or nurturing.

• Getting a flighty nature under control, and bringing one's feet back to terra firma.

• Recognizing and integrating life's stages and cycles positively.

• Improving the health of and yield from your garden, window boxes or groves.

• Extending healthful energy to the land near your home or the entire planet (e.g. land and seed blessings).

• Helping to restore the sacred energy lines of any area.

• Building concrete thought processes that improve your performance at work.

• Matters of abundance and fertility both literal and figurative.

• Cultivating or maturating personal attributes.

Earth Spirits

In the interest of not repeating information, please refer to Chapter Two, and the introductory section to Spirits in "Water" for some guidelines to contacting and working with spirits.

Ao: The four dragon kings of China who are responsible for the four corners of the earth and creation.

Akupera: The Hindu tortoise whose back supports the world.

Bergbui and Bergriser: Teutonic mountain and cliff giants, respectively.

Clio: One of the Greek muses who is the spirit of history.

Dactyls: Greek earth spirits born from Rhea's finger prints.

Fauns: Roman Satyrs who act as companions to Bacchus. They love music, fun and wine.

Gwynn ap nudd: Welsh king of the subterranean fey.

Kubera & Sarvabhauma: Hindu guardian of the northern regions and its protective elephant who supports that part of the world, respectively.

Merlin: Arthurian spirit of the fairy religion and great druid.

Nordhri: Norse dwarf who rules over the ice and the Northern quarter of creation.

Nymphs: Greek. The **oreads** are mountain dwelling nymphs, **Alsaeid** live in the woods and valleys, and the **dryads** live in the forest. Oak leaves are appropriate decorations in the sacred space, especially for the **dryads**.

Onatha: Iroquois Spirit of the Wheat, whose mother was the Earth.

Ovda: Finish forest spirit who is thought to behave quite unpleasantly toward those who cross his path.

Pan: African son of the earth and spirit of cultivation.

P'an-ku: The semi-divine first man of Chinese myths whose body became the foundation of the earth. His head was the cardinal mountain of the East, his arms the south and north, and his feet the west. His belly was the center point of the world.

Ribhus: Hindu elves who oversee crops, specifically herbs.

Sand Altar Woman: Hopi earth spirit who protects in childbirth and guards game animals.

Satyrs & Sileni: Forest and mountain dwelling spirits considered a type of wood genie in Greek tradition. They love pleasure and passion, being brothers to the nymphs and companions to **Dionysus**.

Simargl: Slavic guardian of every seed and plant type.

Tzaphkiel: Angel of 32nd path of Qabala who presides over nature and represents the World card of the Tarot.

Waboose: Native American guardian spirit of the North.

Earth Deities

Please remember that this list, and the preceding one, is but a small representation of the world's Earth-centered spirits, gods and goddesses. For further ideas on figures to supplicate for aid in your magic, please refer to good mythological guides, like Bullfinch.

Adon: Middle Eastern god of corn, the harvest and natural cycles. His sacred animal is a boar.

Aleyin: Phoenician god of vegetation. Offer him libations of rain water.

Amen: Egyptian god of agriculture and fertility whose sacred animals are the ram and goose.

Coatlicue: Ancient Aztec earth and mother goddess. Her sacred symbols include feathers and serpents.

Cronus: Greek god of abundance and earth's riches. Honor him with an hourglass or other emblems of time.

Cybele: Phrygian goddess of earth. Offer her honey and pomegranate seeds, and burn pine or violet incense.

Demeter: Greek personification of fertile or cultivated soil. Appropriate offerings include fruit and corn. Images for the sacred space: dolphin, dove, horse and serpent.

Dhara: Hindu divine being who personifies the earth and attends Indra.

Diana: Roman goddess of nature. Her sacred animals are the dog and elephant.

Dionysus: God of vegetation and moist loam. Honor him in the magic circle with a libation of wine.

Dumuzi: Mesopotamian god of vegetation, fertility and the harvest.

Eithinoha: Iroquois nurturing Mother goddess.

El: Canaan god of earth's fertility whose sacred animal was a bull.

Gaea: Greek goddess whose name means "most ancient earth." Barley and laurel are sacred to her.

Ga-Tum-Dug: Earth mother and creative principle in Assyro-Babylonian tradition.

Geshtin: Assyrian goddess of gardens and vegetation. Decorate your space with grape vines and use grape juice or wine in the ritual cup.

Hawthor: Egyptian mother goddess and personification of nature. Honor her in the sacred space with fresh flowers and libations of wine or ale.

Herne: The Celtic nature god, sometimes confused or blended with cerrenunos.

Hu-Tu: Chinese earth empress whose festival was the summer solstice. Have a square piece of marble on the altar to welcome her.

Isis: Egyptian goddess personifying the female aspects of nature and motherhood. Any harvest items are appropriate as offerings.

Jana: Roman Goddess of the woodlands who protects all the creatures that dwell therein.

Jord: Teutonic earth goddess, and mother to Odin.

Keb: An Egyptian earth god.

Ki: Early Sumerian earth mother who, along with her son Enlil, gave birth to all living things of the planet. Later her aspects became associated with other earth and fertility goddesses - **Ninmah**, **Ninhursag** and **Nammu**.

Kubera: Indian earth god who appears as a dwarf, and guards the treasures of the earth. His sacred numbers are 3 and 8, and suitable offerings include minerals or a silver coin.

Kupila: Russian god of the abundant harvest and earth's fruits.

Luonnotar: A Finish goddess, whose name means "daughter of nature." With the help of a bird (a duck or eagle) luonnotar gave birth to the world after seven centuries of waiting.

Mati Syra Zemlya: Slavic moist earth mother who presides over agricultural fertility, oaths, and property disputes.

Any crops are appropriate to the sacred space.

Mother of Metsola: The Finish personification of the forest.

Mut: Self created world-mother whose sacred animals include the cow and cat.

Nati-syra Zemlya: Slavonic moist earth mother and protectress from malevolent magic and storms.

Nisuba: Assyro-Babylonian goddess of earth's abundance and the harvest. Leave her an offering of grain.

Nokomis: Algonquin earth mother whose bosom feeds plants, animals and people.

O-kuni-nushi: Japanese great land-master god.

Osiris: Nature god, specifically over corn and vegetation. Also the god of growth and stability. Holy numbers are 7, 14 and 28; decorate the sacred space with ostrich feathers.

Pan: Greek god of the woodlands to whom all forest creatures are sacred.

Pellervoinen: Finno-Ugric god who protects fields, and is lord over trees and plants.

Proserpina: Roman grain maiden who also oversees the seasons. Decorate your altar with pomegranates.

Ptah: Ancient Egyptian earth god who is depicted as dwarfish in appearance.

Rhea: Greek earth goddess who created the olympian gods. She was later merged with Cybele. Worship her on mountain tops, or have lion images in the sacred space.

Saturn: Oman god of earthly abundance. Honor him on

12/17 with coins, corn and joyful festivities.

Seb: God of the fertile earth; decorate the sacred space with any farm crops.

Seker: Egyptian vegetation god and god of the dead. His sacred animal is a Hawk.

Seket: Egyptian goddess of cultivated fields. Her color is red, so use this hue in abundance for decorating.

Spenta Armaiti: Persian-Zoroastrian earth goddess who embodies the attributes of Devotion and harmony. Her sacred flower is the musk.

Tammuz: Assyro-Babylonian god of vegetation. Tree twigs or leaves are a good decoration for the sacred space.

Tapio: Finno-Ugric god of mosses and the deep woods along with his wife, son and daughter. Game animals are sacred to him.

Tellus Mater: Ancient Roman earth goddess to whom fruits, flowers and fertile soil are sacred.

Varahavatara: The wild boar avatar of Vishnu whose actions birthed the earth.

Correspondence List

ANIMALS & INSECTS: Most reptiles or creatures that make their home in, or beneath the ground. Ant, badger, bear, bison, buffalo, bull, cat (domestic), caterpillar, cow, deer, dog, donkey, elephant, fox, goat (also air), hedgehog, horse, mouse, pig, rabbit, raccoon, sheep, snake, stag, tortoise, turtle, White Buffalo (Native American).

APPLICATIONS: Cycles, growth, law, money matters, physicality, prosperity, stability, success, sustenance, work-related matters.

ARCHANGEL: Uriel or Gabriel.

ASTROLOGICAL SIGNS: Taurus, Virgo, Capricorn.

CELESTIAL INFLUENCE: The Earth's cycles, the Sun. Venus, Saturn.

COLORS: Black (Celtic, Enochian, China, Navaho, Cheyenne), White (Mayan, Native American, Zuni), Red (Mexico).

CRYSTALS, MINERALS, STONES: Alum, cat's eye, chrysoprase, coal, emerald, flint (also fire), green agate, green calcite, jasper (brown and green), jet, kunzite, lead, malachite, mercury, moss agate, olivine, rock crystal, salt, stalagmite & stalactite, Tourmaline (Green and black), Turquoise (also water due to blue color). Mined items.

DIRECTION: Traditionally North. West (Mexico).

EMBLEMS: Ball, circles, crystals, gems, globe, green or brown items, salt, soil, trees, minerals, metals, pebbles, potted plants, roots or root crops.

FOOD ITEMS (Misc): Barley, brazil nut, buckwheat meal, butter, cheese, macadamia, maple syrup, millet, oat, peanut, rice, rye, soy, wheat. Most meats.

FRUITS & VEGETABLES: Alfalfa sprouts, beets, carrots, corn, mushroom (also water), onions (also fire), peas, potato, pumpkin, quince, radishes (also fire), rhubarb, spinach.

GENDER: Feminine.

GREEK SHAPE: Cubical for stability.

HEBRAIC QUARTER: Shemal (also meaning "left").

HERBS: Allspice, benzoin, comfrey, mace, mugwort, patchouly, salt, storax, sorrel, vervain, vetivert.

LOCATIONS: Caves, farmland, fields, groves, mines, planes, standing stone circles, at or near lay lines. Protected habitats and wild, untouched regions where nature has its way.

MOON PHASE: Dark.

MOONS (Folk Names): Flower time Moon (March), Sprouting Grass Moon and Seed Moon (April), Planting Moon (May), Meadow Moon and Hoeing Corn Moon (June), Plant Moon and Ripe Moon (July), Barley Moon and Grain Moon

(August), Oak Moon (December).

PLANTS, TREES, FLOWERS: Cypress, cotton, fern, horsetail, honeysuckle, ivy, magnolia, oak, oleander, primrose, tulip.

SEASON: Winter, as Earth is usually associated with the Northern quarter of creation.

SENSE: Touch.

TATTWAS SYMBOL (INDIA): Prithivi - a yellow square.

TAROT EMBLEMS: Coin, Pentagram, Disk or Gems; The World Card.

TIME: Midnight.

WIND (Name): Boreas (the North Wind).

Dance with us, ye gentle breezes
carry magic to its mark
Dance with life, with hopeful changes
while 'pon this path, I now embark.

Sing to me, ye winds of wonder
tell me of the times gone by
Sing the words of ancient prophets
tell me where my future lies.

Blow full and strong, Brother Zephyr
through my skin, into my heart
Blow away the looming clouds there
through my soul, your power impart.

I hear you chanting forth the moon
I hear you sigh before the morn
I hear you in the wings of eagles
I hear you in the minstrel's horn.

Yet thine is not a spirit captured
'tis free and flowing like the seas
the wind that moves the mighty ocean
is also the breath
that lives in me.

Chapter Five
Air

"What flies forever and rests never?"

— Old Riddle whose answer is "wind."

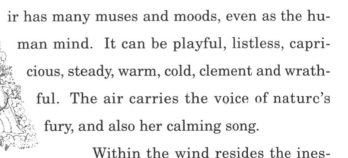

ir has many muses and moods, even as the human mind. It can be playful, listless, capricious, steady, warm, cold, clement and wrathful. The air carries the voice of nature's fury, and also her calming song.

Within the wind resides the inescapable nature of change and entropy, both subtle and potent in its workings. In one moment a full tempest changes one's focus to foundations and security — and not getting too caught up in the moment. In another instance, a vibrant spring zephyr energizes our daydreams and gives them flight. At another time still, a gentle breeze caresses the earth giving us pause to contemplate our body's respiration, which is intimately connected to earth's sigh.

When we breath, air carries vital oxygen to each cell of

our body for renewal and rejuvenation. Within the rhythm of respiration resides the lesson of control and pacing; of knowing when to be still and when to act. Breath, in nearly every esoteric tradition, is also a key component to preparation for meditation. During this stillness, the wind of breath becomes a guiding, regulating spirit, leading to inner-worlds where insight and peace dwell.

On a spiritual level, air represents theoretical ideas and learning, which can often seem just as intangible, not having form until created within the mind. Similarly, air also speaks to us of psychism, those insights and gifts which appear and disappear like a sudden gust of understanding. Within our soul, air becomes the fresh winds that awaken the inner voice, and give it a gentle (or not so gentle) nudge toward expression.

Externally, the Air element is strongly associated with the power of speech and our ability to communicate and network effectively. Our language, its delivery and its subtleties, has an impact that can reach far beyond those who hear our words. We need to use this power wisely. Along with speech, any sound from wind instruments, like the bagpipe or flute, bears the Air element. The spoken word, or such music, may be empowered with Air characteristics by one who knows how to invoke the element. For example, in Mesopotamia, India, Palestine, Egypt and Arabia, mages supplicated the power of Air elemental music to gain power over animals or specific aspects of nature.

In folk tales the subject of catching the wind, or catching a man's breath is used to highlight moral themes about giving people impossible tasks. These stories likely developed due to our progenitor's awe of the wind, and animistic beliefs in its spirit. Such a powerful being, who had no face and no name it chose to reveal would, indeed, be all but impossible to capture, let alone control. Consequently, many magicians consider Air nearly as difficult to master as Fire, definitely having a mind all its own.

Another unique characteristic of Air is the fact that it, like the earth, subtly reflects the other elements. This comes through the four winds. The Northerly wind bears the energies of earth on its chilly arms. The Easterly wind is Air in all its variations. Fire warms the southerly winds, and water dampens those from the West. And with each wind small pieces of other elements get carried from one part of the world to the next in the form of feathers, seeds, leaves, sand, etc. Thanks to these associations and movements, a practitioner can effectively use air as a vehicle for nearly any type of elemental magic, as long as they remember its independent nature.

Myths And Legends

The Bible portrays the element of Air as having a fertile nature ripe to aid in creation. In the beginning, god originated all things with the Word, an expulsion of air with specific, empowered intention. When god's breath moved upon the waters, there was life.

The Phoenicians believed that breath was born of two great principles, and that it existed even before the cosmos.

Other civilizations portray the air as Time's incarnation because time is often elusive, slipping by unnoticed and unappreciated just as the air that we breath. In Greece, writings about Zeus use air or wind analogies to depict this gods' omnipresence.

In Japan, the atmosphere is caused by the wind god's presence, as he lives between heaven and earth. Similar legends elsewhere about primordial air gods depict them as making the earth habitable by separating the Father Heaven from Mother earth. Once separated, this powerful figure holds them apart so animals and humans have room to breath. Some of these gods became the first savior figures.

Legends surrounding the air element are nearly inseparable from that of the winds, as wind gives air specific qualities to which humankind could easily relate. Consequently, personas for each type of wind developed, the Greek myths in particular taking such characterizations to a pinnacle. Here, the empire of the winds was shared between the four sons of Eos (dawn) and Astraeus (the sky). Boreas was the north wind who helped the Argonauts defeat the terrible Harpies, and also dispersed the invading fleet of Zerxes. In human form, Boreas was depicted as a mature man with wings, sometimes with serpent legs.

Prodromes, the north easterly winds, were born from the Harpies when they were slain by Hercules. Their name means "precede" or "forerun" because they appear just before the rise of the Dog Star in this region. Zephyrus was the west wind, who was not always a gentle figure. In early personifications he had

a savage, stormy side that mellowed with age and time to become the beneficial, sweet-scented spring wind. Eurus was the
East Wind, and Notus bore the south winds.

In the Oddessy, Homer also eludes to Aeolus, a guardian
of the winds who could excite or calm them at will. Aeolus lived
in the Aeolian Islands, where he offered hospitality to Odysseus
by giving him a wine skin
which held captive any ill
wind that might threaten
his voyage. Later in his-
tory, Aeolus's image trans-
formed into that of the Father of the Winds, and in
Roman myths he was the
God of Wind.

Air has many muses and moods, even as the human mind.

In American Indian traditions there is a repeated theme
of the wind being a baffling and evasive power that must be har-
nessed so it doesn't overpower humans. The Pueblo and Apache
both speak of the winds abiding at the four quarters of the earth,
and sometimes fighting among themselves for predominance.
This warring helped explain seasonal changes before people understood about the planet's movement.

Finally, the myths of air are also intimately connected
with those surrounding the soul of humankind. In antiquity, a
gust of cold wind was often interpreted as a wandering soul. The
Greeks also postulated that the World Soul (atmos) was contained within the winds. Diogenes of Apollonia hypothesized

that air was the soul and mind in unity, giving life to each creature through breath. Later, this concept translated into the popular notion that the soul departs the body with the last breath to merge with the Infinite.

Folklore, Superstition, Magick

As with the mythology of air, the folklore is also predominated by beliefs about the winds and breath, the first manifestation emanating from nature and the second from humankind.

Animal Lore

• Because of their changeable nature, early peoples believed that chameleons feed off the wind.

Divination

• Some ancient people believed that one could prognosticate by observing the winds and other atmospheric conditions. This type of divination was called aeromancy. One example comes from Greece, where holy people heeded the sound of the wind through the sacred oak trees for their oracles.

• In Tibet people voiced their business questions to the wind then listened. If a crow responded from the Southwest, this was a positive omen of profit.

• Westerly winds in January foretell rain in July, while March and May winds portend a good harvest.

• Cold gusts of wind seeming to originate from nowhere in a home betray the presence of spirits.

• In Chile, people observed the direction in which the winds carried the clouds. If they moved into the south, it portended defeat in war. If they moved to the north, there was reason to rejoice, as any battle plans or those in progress would be victorious.

• Tossing something in the air, then watching to see how it lands, is an old form of divination. Coins are the most commonly known example of this, but other tools were used too, including axes. For the latter, if the point was toward the querent, the answer was "yes," and the point facing away meant "no." I suspect that if the axe missed its mark and hit the querent, this was a definite no!

Fertility

• Warm winds help fertilize hens and mares.

Health

• When someone sneezes, say "God bless you" lest their spirit escape. This tradition began due to the myth that says when Prometheus made man with clay and celestial fire, the body sneezed. Apparently the fire was stolen from the gods, and their wrath was a cold!

• If you have a sickness caused by malevolent magic, burning feathers and releasing the smoke to a wind moving away from you will counteract the magic.

• Night air is dangerous to one's health, so keep your windows closed come dusk. This also keeps any spirits from entering the home, especially those of sickness.

• Tibetan monks disburse sacred sand paintings (mandalas) to the wind as a way of encouraging planetary renewal and well-being.

• In the Middle Ages, cold air was thought to house an evil spirit that could cause illness. Consequently, the mouth was covered when meeting a cold wind to prevent any such spirit from traveling into the body upon inhaling.

Luck

• Before departing on any journey, toss a found coin to the wind as an offering to insure a fortunate adventure.

• If you start out on a new venture or journey and the wind is at your back, this is a sign of good luck to come.

• Catching a leaf loosened by the winds in Autumn before it reaches the ground is very fortunate. It acts as a talisman for luck and well-being through the winter.

• If your luck has been bad of late, and there is a sudden change in the winds, this indicates a change of fortune is at hand.

Weather

• In Rome people called comets "long-haired stars." Their appearance foretold changes in the wind's temperament, usually for the worse.

• To bring a wind when needed, place three knots in a handkerchief. Opening the first knot brings a good sailing breeze, the second stops a tempest, and the last makes the winds calm. Two other techniques were to close a cat up in a room or stick a knife in the mast of a ship (Shetland Islands), both of which inspire the winds.

• In the *Satyricon* (CIV-V) sailors are warned never to cut their nails or hair on ship or it will bring a hurricane. Also one should not whistle on board except when the wind seems to sleep, then it will bring a gentle breeze.

• To protect yourself from harsh winds, carry peony in your pocket. If the winds are serious, burn this flower as an incense to calm the storm.

• It is said that witches can whistle up the wind

• In the southern U.S., black Americans sometimes sang an invocation to the wind to fertilize the rice, give life to a sail, or when a field was being burned.

• In Ireland, a sudden, unexpected gust of wind is believed caused by fairies. This is called a *side gaoite* (fairy wind) or *seidean side* (fairy blast, for whirlwinds). The fairies may either live in such a wind, or cause it by their passing. This is a good omen for hay farmers.

• In the Bahamas, some people believe that hogs can see the wind.

• If traveling by ship, carry beryl with you. This insures favorable winds.

Air Attunement

At first it might seem difficult to become intimately

aware of air in its many forms, but in fact you already have this relationship firmly established in your body thanks to respiration. Without the oxygen transported by each breath, there would not be life. So, begin improving your connection to air by becoming more aware of your breath, of how different types of air feel when you breath of them. Consider: when you inhale, where does it begin? In your chest or diaphragm? Can you feel the air as it moves through your lungs? Also, hold your breath for a moment, then release it. Note how welcome the next fresh breath is to your waiting body, how relaxed and centered it makes you feel once accepted.

Next, start watching your local weather channel when you can in the morning. Try to experience the winds from all four directions, and note how each feels and smells in your journal. Make sure to position yourself so that you face the wind each time for congruity. If you cannot seem to get nature to cooperate in this exercise, try getting an electrical fan and moving it around so that you can experience, in a lesser degree, the missing wind directions. Additionally, try to experience different strengths of wind from each of the four directions (as long as its safe). Your observations will prove most useful to ritual and spell work later.

Learning to heed the wind's voice is far more difficult than the other elements, namely because the delivery and tenor of the words depends on both the direction and ferocity of the air involved. Spring zephyrs murmur gently, sometimes almost imperceptibly, while winter gales howl, making any messages difficult above the din! You will need to spend a fair amount of time with different winds to learn their unique characteristics and undertones. I recommend focusing on one type of wind at a time, honing your awareness to that voice, and then building on that foundational knowledge with other winds. Once you can understand the air, its words of wisdom will surprise you. It will warn of forthcoming changes, reveal undercurrents of situations, whisper bits of foreknowledge and even inspire new ideas.

Air teaches us much about independence and finding our own way, our special own means of effective expression. It also shows that flexibility, being able to move smoothly with and through a situation, is often a powerful and more successful approach than a lot of blustery fanfare. Beyond this the wind reminds us of the responsibility for power, be it invisible or not. The distinction between a strong wind and a tempest probably seems very slight to the Air devas, but the difference in results can equate to life or death in physical reality. Our magic is no different, transporting energy that effects everything with which it comes in contact for boon or bane. Make sure it's controlled properly.

Air Healing

The Air element is very important to nearly all holistic therapies, many of which use a patient's breath as a primary focus for relaxation or vehicle for healing. This is based on the awareness that our breath carries life-giving oxygen to every cell.

Additionally, the symbolism of air as being associated

with freshness, liberation, the season of Spring and day break, creates a potent partnership for wellness.

Aromatherapy

Aromatherapy is a fairly well-known technique that strongly relies on the Air element for its effectiveness. One of the reasons we take flowers to sick people has to do with the virtue of scent carried on the air. Due to this subtle effect, aromatherapy is considered a non-intrusive form of treatment, gently changing, balancing and improving the energies in and around a patient for both physical and emotional results.

Depending on the condition, an aromatic might be added to a potpourri, released to the air via incense, added to hot water or baths, or applied externally to the skin via creams and oils (caution: potent ones like cinnamon may irritate sensitive skin in undiluted form). Some are taken internally to aid conditions, but this is not suggested for the lay person. Essential oils can be very volatile and dangerous if misused.

Here is a brief list of scents that you may wish to try for personal needs. (Please note that this is a very brief overview of a detailed therapeutic approach.) Using these scents certainly won't hurt anything (unless you're allergic), but should not take the place of proper medical examinations and treatments.

Aroma	Conditions
Anise	Colds, flulike symptoms
Bergamot	Depression, anxiety

Aroma	Conditions
Caraway	Digestion
Cedarwood	Chest colds, insect repellent
Chamomile	Bitterness, dissatisfaction, faster healing comfort
Cinnamon	Flu, appetite improvement
Clary	Feminine problems
Clove	Indigestion, energy
Coriander	Fatigue, aggravation
Dill	Stress
Fennel	Nausea, dieting
Geranium	Control anger, stomachache
Grapefruit	Sadness, Ire
Juniper	Menstruation (ease & regulate)
Lavender	Skin problems, rest
Lemon	Cold tonic
Marjoram	Anxiety, asthma
Nutmeg	Aches, insomnia
Peppermint	Stress, flu, mild pain relief
Pine	Inhalant for chest infections
Rose	Confusion, shock
Rosemary	Memory problems, sore muscles
Sage	Infections, swelling
Thyme	Tonic, immunity increase
Violet	Dieting, analgesic

Breath

The importance of breath to our physical well being cannot be overemphasized. One of the reasons that chest colds tend to linger is the fact that they impede the flow of oxygen to our lungs and body which helps keep the healing mechanism of our bodies running smoothly.

More than this, however, breath has an important function in our emotional health too. How often have you heard someone say "take a deep breath and count to ten" in response to someone loosing their temper? The truth is, breathing does help calm over-strained emotions, and can even help heal them. So, whenever you find yourself getting stressed out or flustered — breath! Let the power of air do its work within you.

Casting Sickness to the Wind

Air portable items can be carried or worn on a patient to "collect" the energy of sickness over seven days. Afterwards these get dispersed on the breeze to carry the malady away. Make sure chosen components are earth friendly and not harmful to any living creature that might pick it up. Small seeds are a good choice here, as when they land they can create new life, a very positive image for wellness.

To add more significance to this effort, cast your components into a specific directional wind for more elemental cooperation. Southerly winds work best with colds and chills, Westerly winds work for fevers and soothing a restless mind, Northerly winds are good for long-term problems being that they begin and end the cycle, and working an easterly wind is a good choice for mental disorders, including disorientation and mental exhaustion.

Fanning

Herbs, being burned in a container, may be fanned through a sickroom, house or over the body of a patient to encourage improved energies within the home and their auric field. From a practical standpoint such practices, especially those that use sage and cedar, help inhibit germs while they begin working on the subtle metaphysical level.

The use of feathers is very effective for fanning. These air emblems can also be applied to a patient's auric field to gently balance it out and draw in happier energies (rather like being tickled). To accomplish the latter, begin by drawing the feather along the outer edge of the auric envelope until you feel as if it's smooth. Then slowly move inward, visualizing white, sparkling light pouring through the feather into the aura. This technique requires no incense, but maintains the congruity of the Air element by use of the feather.

Fresh Air

There is an old expression that equates revitalization or new outlooks to "a breath of fresh air." This concept is used quite frequently in folk remedials. As a child, I remember my mother opening the windows even in winter to refresh the house when everyone started getting sick. In earlier times this was done believing the spirit of a sickness needed to leave, but in either case the method often helps.

Beyond this, making sure your living space has good ventilation, and taking walks regularly to get some fresh air are two very practical approaches to wellness. Both provide the additional benefit of giving you time to continue your Air elemental studies and communications.

Air Meditation And Visualization

Individuals who need motivation, a little creative push to inspire their dreams, an improved sense of independence, better clarity in their thought processes, heightened psychic awareness, or improved hope would do well to use the air element as a meditative guide. The type of wind you choose for your meditation should correspond to any goals you have set. For example, creative winds are usually upbeat and lively, independent ones take a tact and stick to it, no matter the obstacles, those for clarity have a brisk edge to stimulate your senses, hopeful ones are warm and gentle, and psychic winds are nearly imperceptible, forcing all our senses to reach out to touch their energy.

As always, however, begin by getting comfortable and centering your attention on the work ahead. When you begin this exercise, the sound of your breathing should be central to your attention. Listen to its rhythm, its special song. Allow yourself to totally relax, noticing how the breath changes as tensions flow away on each exhalation. Once the thoughts of the day have faded to a self-awareness, begin visualizing yourself in

140

a natural setting appropriate to the wind you've chosen. For example, you might see yourself at a beach during summer for the warm, gentle winds that engender renewed faith, or standing on a high mountain peek for the cool winds of precision.

In your visualization, feel the wind meet and greet your skin. Sense its touch, how it energizes your pores. Smell the power of that wind, its unique aroma that also depicts its personality. Taste it, and listen to its message for you. Reach out for it with your hands as if to embrace it,

Learning to heed the wind's voice is far more difficult than the other elements.

taking it into yourself as you continue breathing.

For those who have trouble visualizing this because wind is not visible except by what it affects, add colored light to the wind so you can see it flow naturally into your inner being. This is achieved in two ways: by visualizing the light-air being internalized with your breath, or seeing it absorbed directly through your pores. Make sure you choose the color of light to mirror the intentions of the meditation. Here are correspondences to consider:

Red: Improved energy for manifesting one's dreams, or to give renewed life to hopes that have dwindled in despair.

Orange: Producing effective networking and

communication skills, especially among friends and kin

Yellow: Tuning into your cognitive self, especially in matters of higher learning.

Green: Healing your sense of self, or mental distress.

Blue: A fertile wind that germinates then waters your aspirations.

Purple: Spiritual movement; a renewed awareness of one's spiritual nature and connection to the sacred.

White: Cleansing and rejuvenation of mind and spirit.

Another alternative to this meditation is visualizing yourself as being one with, part of, or as an observer of, anything you personally associate with Air. For example, place yourself on the wings of a bird and let it fly high above your problems to grant new perspectives. Meditate on the windmill that generates energy without ever going or moving out of its circular pattern. Attach your worries to a feather or cloud and let the next good gust blow them neatly away.

Continue your visualization until you feel the work is done. Return to the sound of your breathing, then slowly to an awareness of your surroundings. Make notes as soon as possible in your journal for future reference.

Rituals

Describing the role of the Air element in ritual is a little more difficult than the other elements, simply because another element was usually involved to create the desired effect. For example, in Temples throughout the ancient world, aromatics burned on altars to the gods and goddesses [e.g. the Fire element]. Air carried the scent of these fires to the divine, bearing the prayers of the faithful in the smoke. To this day incense remains an emblem functional for either Fire or Air in the ritual circle! Another example is when sacred emblems are scribed in the air for invocations or protection. In this case the tool used (athame—Fire, wand—Earth) creates the visual image, while the air becomes a spiritual blackboard, holding the images in its elemental matrix.

Among magical practitioners, other emblems of Air include feathers, bells, handheld (or electrical) fans, and images of birds placed in the eastern quarter of the circle. Offerings of aromatic are also still quite acceptable as a way to honor the divine, the aromas chosen to be specifically appropriate to the visage upon whom the practitioner calls. For example, the traditional scent for Apollo is bay; for Demeter, myrrh; for Poseidon , cedar; and for Hawthor, floral aromas. To these basic ingredients others may be added that correspond with the practitioner's goal, like adding frankincense to Demeter's incense when requesting her blessings and protection on one's land.

In air rituals conducted specifically for healing, the perimeter of the circle might be decorated with wind chimes so that rehabilitative sounds encompass the person in need. These should be pleasing and not overly loud so as to not disturb the inner-circle work. At a blessing way ritual, the child can be fanned with the aroma from incense or other aromatic to protect and cleanse the child, and introduce them to the Air element. As a side note here, the old tradition of spanking a baby at birth to get breathing started was, for a time, a kind of ritual that likewise introduced Air in a more mundane setting.

For handfastings, have the couple release a kiss to the southerly wind as a wish for growing love and inspired passion. Finally, to banish negativity, stand with your back to the wind, and walk backwards (mark out the path ahead of time for safety) against it to turn away those energies. Don't forget, when need be an open window or even an air conditioner can act as an air symbol.

Spellcraft

Magically speaking, the direction of wind used in spellcraft is vitally important. From the south it offers cleansing, passion, and energy. From the west comes nurturing, emotions, and insight. From the north we receive rest and renewal after hard labors, and from the east we welcome new beginnings and hope.

To work effectively with the Air element, all components chosen for your spell should be light enough to be carried on a breeze, while still mirroring your intentions. Incense, flower petals, powdered kitchen herbs, seeds, bark shavings, feathers, small bits of recycled paper, fruit rind shavings diced small, and other nearly weightless objects are good examples. Because Air does not have a form easily captured as a component to spellcraft, I have focused mostly on the elements of a spell that might be given to the air/winds herein:

Airing it out: Placing a symbol in direct contact with the wind helps to figuratively air things out that seem to keep getting swept under the proverbial rug. For example, hang the name of a gossiper on the clothesline so the false nature of their words is revealed by their own "hot air," or, better still, hang out the rug so there's no place for deception or avoidance to hide! Another example is opening the windows of your home before having difficult confrontations with people so that fresh winds can offer new, and hopefully better, perspectives.

Aromas: During the Middle Ages, the art of the perfumer was, by some, elevated to the level of spellcraft, usually by the men who succumbed to the charms of the woman wearing the scent. On a more personal level, this means that you can make specially prepared scented oils to wear and accentuate your magical goals no matter where you may be, and give movement to your energy each time that scent is caught by a breeze. For example, when wishing to draw love to you use a rose scent or for improved peace of mind, wear lavender.

Flower Petals: Flower petals are one of the best components for air magic, being very light and having a language all their own thanks to our Victorian ancestors. Match the wind of choice and the flower to your magical intentions for best results.

For example, with the love spell discussed above, release rose petals with your wish, then anoint yourself with the oils. Or, for the peace spell, shower yourself with the lavender so that calmness falls over you like a balm, then apply the scented oil.

Knots: Several classical sources including Shakespeare and the Oddessy talk of the use of knots to capture the power of air in a conveniently carried item. The Corsairs were also reported to use wind knots to aid their sailing, often purchased in Arabic ports. To create an air rope for your magic, take it outside when the wind is blowing a favorable direction for your magical goals. Hold the rope to the air and begin tying three knots saying "Within thee bind, the wind is mine." Once completed the air rope can be used mundanely to bring a breeze on a particularly hot day by opening one of the knots. It may also be used to bring the air element when you need it for magic. Please note however, that it is traditional never to open the third knot; this brings a tempest to those who get greedy!

Seeds: Another light object that engenders fertility, gestation, and growth once it reaches its location. Consider seeds mingled with the air element for aiding personal inventiveness (e.g. the "seeds" of imagination), learning the benefits to patience, or any matters which require change or movement so maturity can come.

Shouting into the Wind: Many ancient civilizations

knew well the power of the spoken word. The ancient samurai, for example, used the kai (or shout of power) before attacking an enemy. This shout not only served to frighten the intended, but also focused energy within the warrior to the task ahead. Using this concept, one might wish to shout their wishes into an appropriate wind to carry that desire and energy not only to the Universe, but also back to your own heart. For improved results, repeat the word or phrase a symbolic number of times (Once for unity; twice for partnerships and balance; thrice for the trinity of mind-body-spirit; Four times for solidarity, etc.).

Windy Release: Tie an object that represents your magical goal loosely in a tree or other area where the wind can reach it. Add a verbal component if desired. When the object is naturally taken by the air, your spell will begin to manifest.

Holiday Observances

The holiday observances which correspond to the Air element are either those whose theme matches the applications given for Air, those who celebrate or predict the winds, or those which somehow revere Air animals.

1/1 New Year's Day: Open a window today and welcome the winds of luck and health.

1/7 Carnival: A day filled with joyful freedom and revelry. Bolivian dancers wear plumed costumes as part of their festival.

1/12 Festival of Sarasvati: Hindu celebration to honor

this goddess whose sacred animals are the swan and peacock. Sarasvati is invoked for creativity especially on writing projects.

1/25 St. Paul's Day: If it is windy today, it foretells misunderstandings, difficulties and even possibly war.

2/14 Valentine's Day: According to popular lore, birds choose mates today.

2/28 Kalevala Day: Finish festival remembering the importance of oral tradition in the keeping of their people's stories and epics.

Late March: Passover. Celebrate the spirit of liberation in your life.

3/25 Hilaria: Roman festival were laughter is truly the best medicine. Release your tensions to a cool gust of air, and laugh heartily.

3/27 Smell the Breeze Day: Egyptian festival during which it is beneficial to go outside and get some fresh air.

4/1 April Fool's Day: Truly a day to celebrate your inner child and loose some restrictions in your life.

4/5 Kwan Yin Day: Chinese and Japanese festival for this goddess of prophesy. Also a kite festival!

4/8 Birthday of Buddha: In Thailand people often release captive birds today to honor Buddha's teachings.

5/5 Feast of Banners & Kites: Banners and kites are given to the winds everywhere today in Japan celebrating masculine attributes.

6/4 Rosiala: Ancient Greeks burned rose incense on the winds today for luck and to honor Aphrodite.

6/17 Cleansing Lily: Japanese people take to the streets waiving tiger lilies to supplicate the spirits for dry air.

7/12 Good Luck Day: European festival during which any new endeavors or travels will be met with good fortune.

8/9 Festival of the Milky Way: Chinese people believe that once a year magpies build a winged bridge for a herdsman who loves the Sun god's daughter so he can see her.

8/18 Eisteddfod: Welsh druidic gathering during which new bards are chosen, and runes are read. A good time to reinforce your communication or divination skills.

9/21 St. Mathews Day: Fair winds today ported four more weeks of pleasant weather.

10/12 Fortuna Redux: Roman observance for this patroness of travel, especially for sailing journeys which receive gentle winds.

11/20 Makahiki Hawaiian festival that coincides with the appearance of the Pleadies in the sky. According to tradition these stars were once fairies who flew to the sky to escape Orion's passions.

The Muses of Greece may have been a type of sylph.

Early December Dervish Dancing: The whirling dervishes wear skirts that catch the air so they become the center of life's circle. After sacred spinning dances, they become oracles, providing divinations to those gathered.

12/14 Hopi Winter Ceremony: It is traditional to make a feathered prayer stick during this rite as a wish for a gentle voice.

12/25 Yule: The ashes from the yule log should be sprinkled to the winds around your house to bring blessings back on the air.

Working With Air Devas

The fourth class of devas, called Sylphs, live in a middle region that is less tangible than earth's atmosphere. The ancients held that the sylphs were directly responsible for many oracles, bearing messages from the heavens on their wings. This includes the famous oracle at Donada, whose sacred oak leaves were moved by the winds generated by these beings.

Sylphs often work cooperatively with the other elements. For example, they join with the Undines for designing snow flakes and gathering rain clouds. Similarly, they may aid earth devas with fertilization by providing winds filled with seeds and pollen.

Sylphs ride on breezes and are considered the highest of the elementals in their vibrational rate. No matter their age, these creatures never look old, in natural or human form. Most often they appear as having a feminine visage, probably because of their less solid, diaphanous consistency which has a gentle and lovely form when seen.

The word sylph comes from a word meaning butterfly. As one might expect from such an association, the sylphs have a similarly flittery disposition filled with mirth and capriciousness. They do not like being confined or restricted in any way, having a fierce sense of independence, but do enjoy teaching humans who have an open mind on various topics under their domain.

The Muses of Greece may have been a type of sylph, gathering in the creative essence of a dreamer's mind and further inspiring them toward beauty. People who have a keen wit and sparkling personality will attract these creatures quite naturally, as the sylphs love intelligence, good humor, upbeat perspectives and vibrancy. Sylphs also seem to naturally love pets and children, with innocent, trusting demeanors.

Appropriate requests for Air devas include:
- Inspiring a connection with, and understanding of, your inner child
- Increasing youthful zeal and energy for a new project
- Improving spiritual insights
- Motivating psychic gifts toward manifestation
- Providing fresh ideas to help a project that lost its vibrancy
- Traveling safely, especially by air
- Comprehending of theoretical material, especially esoteric
- Smoothing transitions; helping you move with life
- Sending the winds of love, luck or playfulness into your life

- Freeing one's imagination and creative spirit to soar

- Learning to speak, listen and hear effectively

- Releasing your mind from old, outmoded thought forms

Air Spirits

More so than any other element, the Air spirits are unpredictable and impulsive. They also tend to take less kindly to those who would try to command or ensnare them. Consequently, these spirits should be consulted with all due caution.

Ambriel: Archangel of the 17th Sephirah of the Qabala who oversees the lungs, prophetic ability and messages from the Higher Self.

Austri: Nordic dwarf who rules the air and the Eastern portion of creation.

Boreas: Greek personification of the North wind who assisted the Athenians in the Persian war by destroying enemy ships. Boreas's emblem was a conch shell.

Cloud People: Pueblo spirits who live in the four regions of the universe, and with whom the spirits of the dead are associated.

Euterpe: Greek Muse of flute playing whose music mirrored that of the heavenly spheres. Also presided over memory.

Gabriel: Archangel of the 9th Sephirah of the Qabala, presiding over change, divinatory arts and the intuitive nature.

Ga-Oh: Seneca Indian spirit of the four winds who lives

in the North, and controls the seasons. Before his home are four guardians; a bear representing the North wind, a panther representing the west wind, a fawn representing the south wind, and a moose representing the east wind.

Gremlin: A troublesome airborne being, impish in character and very strong. While many similar creatures are discussed in folklore, the word itself was popularized in 1922, during World War 1 by a British Air Commission pilot, whose name has not been released.

Harpie: Greek tempest spirits and winged monsters. The word harpie means to "seize" probably due to their reputation for trying to steal food and cause famine.

Indra & Airavata: Hindu guardian of the eastern world and elephant protector who supports that quarter of creation, respectively.

Kari: Teutonic giant of the air.

Kliwa: A Taos Indian terrible wind spirit that brings sickness, specifically epidemics.

Michael: Archangel of the 8th Sephirah of the Qabala watching over spiritual contact with guides, safe travel and matters of learning.

Raphael: Archangel of the 11th Sephirah of the Qabala overseeing the spirit of ether and the superconscious.

Thunder: Among the plains Indians, the most important of all air spirits whose voice is that of the Great Spirit. This being is personified by a giant bird (the thunder bird).

Typhoeus: Spirit of the hurricane in Greek mythology.

Tzaphkiel: Archangel of the 3rd Sephirah of the Qabala who stabilizes thought and aids in matters of faith.

Wabun: Native American Spirit Keeper of the east.

Whirlwind, The: A personified spirit among certain Southwestern Indian tribes, often of a deceased person. Generally it is considered a bad omen to come in contact with this phenomena.

Wind Old Man: Taos Pueblo spirit, now believed to have dissipated its power or the winds would be far worse.

Wind Old Woman: Pueblo spirit who lives in the center of the world receiving offerings from those suffering from rheumatism.

Air Deities

Addad: Assyro-Babylonian master of the storm and tempest, who also brings beneficent winds and rain. Lord of foresight.

Aditi: Indian god of the sky and air. Also the god presiding over the Aryan nations, who knows the past and future.

Amun: Egyptian Great Father with a ram's head and a crown of plumage. He ruled over the wind, air, prophesy and fertility.

Anila: Hindu divine being who personifies the wind and is an attendant to Indra.

Anubis: Egyptian god of intelligence, journeys, and astral travel. His sacred animal is a dog or jackal.

Artemis: Greek patroness of singers, psychism, and good

travel. A suitable emblem for her is a silver acorn.

Baal: Canaanite god of the atmosphere.

Bast: Egyptian cat goddess who embodies joy and playfulness. Honor her in the sacred space with wine and flute music.

Chiquinau: Nicaraguan god of the nine winds and the air.

Desire: Phoenician dark wind of chaos that mingled upon itself to become the principle of creation. Here, Desire and Darkness gave birth to Aer (air) and Aura (breath), equating to intelligence and the first living creature, respectively.

Ecalchot: Nicaraguan wind god who lived in the eastern portion of creation with the Creators themselves.

Enlil: Assyro-Babylonian Lord of the winds.

Feng-po: Chinese Earl of the Wind who carried a goatskin bottle from which the winds pour forth.

Feng P'o P'o: A kindly old woman in Chinese mythology who replaced Feng-po later in history as the ruler of the winds. Sometimes depicted as moving among the clouds on the back of a great tiger.

Haya-ji: Japanese god of the whirlwind.

Hermes: Greek messenger of the gods with winged feet. Hermes controlled the winds, the four seasons, mischief, travel and philosophy.

Ilmarinen: Finnish god of the wind and good weather.

Marduk: Mesopotamian god of the winds and hurricane. Appropriate emblems for him include a ring, rod, dagger or bull.

Meuler: Araucanian (Chile) god of the winds, specifically whirlwinds and those that carry water.

Mixcoatl: Aztec cloud serpent whose sacred animals include deer and rabbits.

Nabu: Mesopotamian god of speech and the intellect. His sacred animals are the dragon or serpent.

Nanshe: Assyrian goddess of awareness, prophesy and the interpreter of dreams. Her symbol is a cup into which her devotees gazed for divinatory insights.

Nephthys: The "revealing" goddess, depicted with winged arms. She oversees dreams, the intuitive nature, and hidden things. Decorate the circle with shades of green, and have a basket somewhere in the sacred space.

Ninurta: Sumerian god of the south wind to whom amethyst or lapis are both suitable offerings.

Nuit: Egyptian sky goddess to whom all winged creatures are sacred.

Set: Egyptian storm god (also mist and rain) whose sacred animals include the antelope, black pigs, boar and ass.

Shina-Tsu-Hiko: Japanese god of the wind who blew away the mist that covered the land and created the goddess, Shina-to-Be.

Shu: Egyptian god of air and emptiness, whose name means "to raise." An ostrich feather creates an ideogram of his name.

Stribog: Slavonic wind god who causes the noise in storms along with Erisvorsh, the tempest.

Tatsuta-Hiko and Tatsuta-Hime: Japanese wind god and goddess to whom people pray for good harvests, and whose

"Air" by Colleen Koziara

visage fishermen wear to protect themselves from storms.

Thoth: Egyptian god of learning, beginnings, invention and oratory skills. Offer him sweetmeats, honey or figs.

Vayu: The Vedic god of the wind and atmosphere; the breath of life residing in the North West corner of creation. His sacred animal is the antelope.

Yazata: Iranian gentle wind god.

Zeus: Greek great God over all high things, including the wind, mountain tops, and matters of luck. His sacred tree is the oak, through which oracles were interpreted.

Correspondence List

ANIMALS & INSECTS: Most birds and winged creatures; also those that dwell in high windy regions. Antelope, bat, beetle, bobcat, butterfly, chameleon, dragonfly, eagle (Native American), flying fish (also water), tree squirrels or snakes, spider in a web. The dolphin and whale as emblems of the breath of life.

APPLICATIONS: Beginnings, communication, freedom, imagination, love, luck, transition, understanding, the mental plane of thought & ideas, abstract knowledge, psychism and prophesy, travel and movement, youthful outlooks and the inner child.

ARCHANGEL: Raphael or Michael.

158

ASTROLOGICAL SIGNS: Gemini, Libra, Aquarius.

CELESTIAL INFLUENCES: Mercury, Jupiter.

COLORS: Red (Celtic, Enochian, Mayan, Cheyenne), Blue (Mexico), White or Green (China), Yellow (Native American, Zuni), White (Navaho).

CRYSTALS, MINERALS, STONES: Aluminum, aventurine, copper, jasper, mercury, mica, pumice, sphene, tin, topaz. Additionally or optionally any crystal, mineral or stone with yellow, white or very pale blue coloring.

DIRECTION: Traditionally East. South (Mexico).

EMBLEMS: Athame, bells, censer, clouds, electrical or hand-held fans, feathers, flower petals, kites, an open window, pinwheel, potpourri, smoke, wind chimes.

FOOD ITEMS (MISC): Almond, bamboo shoots, bergamot tea, brazil nuts, chestnut, chicory, hazelnut, honey, maple syrup, olive, parsley, pecans, pine nuts, pistachio, rice. Anything dehydrated by exposure to air.

FRUITS & VEGETABLES: Banana, beans, citron, date, endive, kumquat, mulberry, parsley, tangerine.

GENDER: Masculine.

GREEK SHAPE: Octahedral as in intermediary between water and fire.

HEBRAIC QUARTER: Kedem, which also means "front."

HERBS: Anise, bergamot, bittersweet, caraway, chicory, frankincense, lemon grass, lemon verbena, myrrh, mace, marjoram, mint, oregano, peppermint, sage, savory, turmeric, vervain, yarrow.

LOCATIONS: Any area that accentuates the wind like cliff sides, mountain tops, plains, beaches, peaks, towers.

MOON PHASE: Waning.

MOONS (Folk Names): Wind Moon (February), Stormy Wind Moon and Crow Moon (March), Wild Goose Moon and Big Wind Moon (April), Mild Weather Moon (June), Little Wind Moon (September), Moon of Falling Leaves (October).

PLANTS, TREES, FLOWERS: Aspen, borage, broom, bamboo, clover, dandelion, goldenrod, hops, ironwood, lavender, linden, male fern, meadowsweet, mistletoe, palm, pansy, pine, primrose, slippery elm, violet.

SEASON: Spring.

SENSE: Smell.

TIME: Dawn; the hour of renewed hopefulness.

TATTWAS SYMBOL (INDIA): Vayu - a blue circle.

TAROT REPRESENTATION: Rod, wand, staff. Also the Chariot (for movement), the Hanged Man whose life is "up in the air" and potentially the Star for its hopeful message.

WIND (name): Eurus (the East Wind).

"Fire" by Colleen Koziara

Burn within
spark of creation
coals of Spirit
ye kindling for magic

Purifying flames
whose pyres create beauty
from destruction
wellness from dis-ease
hope from embers
and light from the night
pray, burn.

Essence of the morning star
Father-Son-Lover in glory
Power over darkness
illuminate also our hearts.

Place therein the fire of truth
the flaming arrow of justice
the red spear of righteousness
and the gold shield of courage
with which to walk surely
the Path of Beauty
forever.

Chapter Six
Fire

"The more you feed it, the more it grows high, but if
you give it water, it will surely die.
> *— Old Riddle whose answer is "fire."*

"A hill full, a whole full, but you cannot
catch a bowlful."
> *— Riddle whose answer is "smoke."*

he first representation of fire that was most
significant to early people was the sun.
This blazing daily visitor banished the dangerous darkness, seeming to chase it back into itself. The awe this inspired eventually mani-
fested in sun worship, and sun gods and god-
desses appearing in nearly every culture. With this in mind, it is
understandable why fire would also become a venerated ele-

ment. It looked as if it came from the same divine source that burned in the sky, it gave off warmth, and better yet gave light to the night even when the sun was sleeping!

As an element, Fire is purifying, empowering, creative and destructive. Like a sword or any blade, it bears two distinct edges. One is the warmth of a well-tended fire offering kinship, safety and companionship to all who gather there. The other is a terrible, destructive force that burns everything in its path, then goes out, completely expended. With this in mind, it is understandable why among shamans learning control over this element is one of the last steps toward spiritual mastery. One cannot connect with this element without risking getting burned both literally and figuratively.

Fire has a purgative nature that found its ultimate representation in cremation, as evidenced in diverse regions ranging from Russia and Scandinavia to the Archipelago. Among Native Americans especially, cremation is perceived as a way of releasing the spirit for its next life, the fire marking the passage from the material to the immaterial worlds, and the spirit being likened to something as liberated and intangible as smoke.

In East Africa, cremation is one way religious leaders free ghosts from a body so they can enter the spiritual realm (and hopefully thereby leave the living in peace). Additionally, for the believer the burning process creates a connection with the Divine while neatly severing any remaining ties the spirit has to animal totems and the mundane world. For the living, the visual impact should not be overlooked either, the fire consuming the last vestige of the image associated with that person. In some modern instances, the presence of torches or candles at wakes and burials are substitutes for, or contemporary variations on, the cremation rite. Part of the light here also represents the soul, and the Spirit to which it returns.

In the body, Fire manifests in the beating of our heart and in the physical warmth which creates the auric envelope. Additionally, the region of the heart chakra is often de-

In Iran, for example, there are five ritual fires.

picted as a flame that looks strikingly similar to a DNA helix. This is no coincidence, since spiritually speaking the pattern of our true self, our soul and all its learning, resides within the heart chakra. Additionally, DNA is the paradigm of the life spark as we know it.

Within one's home, Fire is the hearth and heart. Among Armenians, for example, someone getting a new home away from their family for the first time always takes fire from the family hearth with them to light their fireplace (or more modernly the pilot light). This action symbolically keeps the family united, and transports love to the new residence. Similarly, in ancient Greece, people lit a new colony's fire from that of the public hearth in the mother city to show unity. In this manner, fire not only symbolizes the continuance of civilization or families from one generation to the next, but also the continuance of honored traditions, loyalty to one's place of origin, and kinship. Thus, light became a binding tie in the ancient world moving from hand to hand, marking new beginnings and human expansion.

In the Temple, the Fire element becomes the sacred flame honoring the divine presence therein. Traditionally this fire is made totally fresh after the sacred space is erected. Before lighting the fire, all other nearby fires must be extinguished in tribute. This particular custom intimates that early peoples regarded fire as holy and as having a godly spark within. This allusion is definitely mirrored in the myths and legends of numerous cultures.

Myths And Legends

Several themes reoccur in the myths surrounding fire, the most predominant of which is that fire is a divine element stolen or borrowed from either the sun itself or another divine visage. For example, in Brazil there is the story of an old man who stole fire from the vultures and hid it in the trees (wood being the predominant source of early fires). In Greek tradition, Prometheus brings fire to Earth on a fennel stalk and gives it to humankind who sneezes upon its receipt. Why? Because Prometheus stole the sacred flame, and apparently colds became the divine retribution to humankind for accepting such a powerful gift without question.

The stories from oceanic cultures mirror these motifs in

167

several ways. Again we see fire being borrowed or stolen from its owner by humankind. Who owns this fire, where they dwell and who finally retrieves it are the story components that vary from island to island. In some cases the fire comes down from heaven, while in others it is brought up from the lower worlds. No matter its origin, however, in all cases the person retrieving the fire must guard it with care, never letting it go out. The implied result of such negligence is nothing less than disaster for that race.

A secondary theme for the Fire element occurs among the legends of smith and fire gods like Hephaestus and Wayland. Many of these personas are featured as crippled. Hephaestus incurred his injuries when he fell from heaven, for example. Presumably such stories are moralistic fables that reveal the two-edged nature of Fire. Mastery of this element

As an element, Fire is purifying, empowering, creative and destructive.

seems often times to carry a high price.

In some instances myths indicate that fire came to earth quite by accident. In the Congo and New Guinea, people discovered it while sawing. In another story, a Creator god angered by a bird threw a burning log at it. The log missed and fire fell to earth. Again, in Finland, the supreme god Ukko ignited fire when his flaming sword struck a fingernail. Although he confided this special spark to the virgin of the air, she let it escape. It rolled through the clouds, fell into a lake, was eaten by a trout, who got consumed by a salmon, who in turn got eaten by a pike. It was then, finally, that the chief hero of the Finish sagas, Vainamoinen, catches the pike, frees the spark, and eventually captures it in a copper jar beneath a birch stump!

In ancient Persia people revered fire as the epitome of life's force, virtue, purity and illumination. This outlook was not unusual, however. Nearly every ancient civilization revered the light of a fire for its protection and warmth, not to mention its utilitarian value. Likewise, as mentioned at the beginning of this chapter, the ball of fire above (the sun) was worshipped as a Divine figure, so it seemed natural that earthly fire would follow suit.

Biblically the idea of light/fire as being divine translated into the Holy Spirit who descended upon worshippers with "tongues of fire." In the Old and New Testament, this aspect of the trinity often appears as a blazing white-light, like the purest of fires. As an interesting aside, in Hebrew tradition Yahweh was a master of fire.

The child of fire, namely ash, also has some interesting mythology associated with it. In the cosmology of Mocovi, ashes from a celestial tree created the Milky Way. The Incans believe that, in jealousy, the sun once threw ashes on the moon to keep it from shining brightly, which is why it is now grey in color. Among the Aztec, humankind was created from ashes, in Arabian folk tales people are often reduced to ashes magically, and in the traditional tale of the Phoenix, this great bird rises from its own ashes totally renewed. These tales, and others like them give fire the symbolism of generative force, annihilation and complete renewal or resurrection.

Folklore & Superstition

As one might expect, fire was terribly important to our ancestors being that it not only provided heat and safety, but aided in creating what would eventually become small societies. Each night, gathering around a fire developed into a clan ritual, which still has significance today at meal time!

Beyond this, however, fire symbolized the life-giving power of the sun which greeted people each day offering a welcome change from the darkness. Consequently, fire lore also includes beliefs about the sun and its effects, alongside beliefs about physical fires.

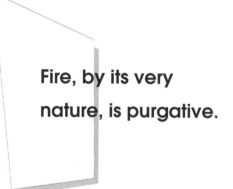

Fire, by its very nature, is purgative.

Abundance

• If lightning (fire from the sky) strikes on the 27th day of the month, the harvest will be plentiful, but poor if it strikes on the 29th.

• When the sun shines on any occasion it is a sign of divine blessings and abundance to come.

• Jumping over the Balefire (Beltane) is said to bring the participant fertility, health and plenty.

Divination

• A sparking fire announces a letter's arrival, a baby, or marriage on the horizon.

• Soot falling from a chimney is an omen of important news.

• A sizzling fire warns of arguments in the home or a forthcoming storm.

• Tall flames in a fire mean that a relative or friend is thinking fondly of you.

• A fire that burns blue indicates the presence of spirits, as does one that dances without sign of a wind.

• The patterns created by sparks and soot from the hearth fire may be interpreted for portents. For example, seeing a heart foretells love.

• A fire that blazes suddenly announces the arrival of a stranger.

• Fires that burn black and smoky indicate dissention in one's home.

• Fires that spit and roar reveal a superior's displeasure with you, or tell of someone spreading gossip.

• If you toss a sprig of your hair on the fire and it burns brightly, you will live a long, healthy life.

• If you gaze at a candle's flame while thinking of a question, the flame's movement will provide an answer. Bright, active movement is a positive portent, while smoldering or going out is negative.

• Candles that burn down only on one side forming a winding sheet foretell a death that year.

• A smoking fire indicates the presence of an invisible witch in the house.

• A hearth fire which burns on only one side presages an engagement or marriage.

Love

• Never allow the hearth fires of a home to go out or love will also disappear. Modernly this might equate to a pilot light, or even a small light bulb left burning in a safe place. When the bulb needs changing, turn on another light source temporarily to maintain congruity of the symbol.

• To keep friendships true, never poke at the hearth of another; this brings strife.

Luck

• Never tamper with the hearth fire at another home. This insults the house spirit and brings bad luck.

• Jumping over a St. John's fire purifies the participant and brings them improved luck.

• Pebbles formed by a lightning strike often look like arrowheads or hatchets, and are considered lucky talismans.

• Burning a candle at dawn on Christmas day brings luck.

• Do not stir your Yule fire during meal time or ill fortune will follow.

• Give a baby a gift of matches so they will always have warmth and luck throughout their life.

• It is very bad luck to let the hearth fires go out on New Years, Beltane, Hallows and Midsummer's because this is when both fairies and spirits are most active.

• To insure good fortune with your baking projects, and continued luck for the family, do all your cooking and food passing in a sunwise (clockwise) direction.

• The belief that it is unlucky to open an umbrella in the house comes from the fact that it is a sun-wheel emblem. To open it outside of the sun's domain incurred the wrath of this powerful being.

• Tribal people felt it was essential to have an ever-burning fire to insure continued blessings and fortunes. When the fire went out, it indicated the loss of life.

• Fires that will not light are very bad luck and should be dismantled. They can draw evil spirits.

Prosperity

• Never light a candle from a fire; this brings poverty.

Protection

• A piece of wood struck by lightning (electrical fire) can protect from fairies on May day, and acts as a safeguard against lightning the rest of the year (e.g. "lightning never strikes twice.")

• Passing animals through the smoke of a Beltane fire protects them from sickness and disease.

Weather

• To keep storms away, throw salt in the fireplace.

• To stop a downpour, quench a fire with water.

• A crackling fire portends a frost soon to come.

• A sulky fire indicates rain in the forecast on the morrow.

Fire Attunement

Fire has several forms, some of which are easier to attune to than others simply because of their intensity (as compared with what a body can endure safely). Some of the easiest types of Fire to begin working with are the flame from a candle, the spark from a match, sun rays, a well tended barbecue fire (made only with natural ingredients), and even potentially more technological light and fire sources like pilots and light bulbs!

Take the time to experience each safe type of Fire that you can, with as many senses as possible. Note the varying heat levels, how different types of light and heat affect your emotions, your body, and more importantly what impressions they give you spiritually. Consider and compare things like the pleasant warmth of a sunny day versus the harsh, angry heat of an overstacked fire. It is also important to see how long different types of fires last, and consider that significance to your work with the element. For example, you would probably not wish to

174

invoke the spirit of a raging fire for aid, as the energy in that spirit will quickly consume itself.

Fire's messages come to us in two different ways, through sight and hearing. Visually the salamanders may form symbolic or literal images within a fire for your insightful eye to discern. Pyromancy is a very ancient art, often centering about the fires in a sacred space, for insights believing that a bit of divine energy was part of the flame. Alternatively, fire may communicate through sparks, hisses and cracks. Generally speaking the more vibrant these are, the more positive the answer. Fire is a very excitable element!

Fire's lessons are several-fold. First it teaches the value of perspective. From earth the sun is warm and welcoming, but if we get too close to that fire, it burns us just as sure as being too close to a difficult situation can "burn" us because clarity is hindered. Secondly, it reminds us that we must balance our magical powers and use the energy therein wisely, or else the potential exists to burn ourselves out. This happens to many metaphysical teachers who don't know how to say "no."

Regulation is another theme from fire's snapping hearth. When camping, a fire provides safety, warmth and a place to cook. However, poorly built ones, or those without proper tending can get out of hand and destroy everything in its path. So, in learning about magic and practicing our faith we need to remember that all things come in their time. Anything worth having is worth consistent effort and care to obtain.

Finally, one of the most important lessons of Fire lay in

its light. Plants grow toward the light of sun, and stretch their reach in any way necessary to reach that source. Similarly, we too should always be stretching toward the divine light who is our maker, and our source.

Fire Healing

Fire by its very nature is purgative. When we get sick, a fever often results as an outward manifestation of the body's battle for wellness. Additionally, according to practitioners, the Fire element is attuned to magnetism upon which reiki and accupressure depend for guidance.

When a normal fire is ignited, the darkness seems to flee backwards from the brightness. This visual effect is potent in healing, figuratively frightening away the shadow of sickness. Likewise, Fire can consume what it touches, allowing dis-ease to be burned away in the flame. The caution here, however, is that too much fire becomes a conflagration, raging out of control to-ward disastrous ends. In metaphysical healing this element must be handled with great care; ours is to help, not harm.

Ashes: The ashes from Sacred fires (those built in honor of a divine figure) have figured into numerous forms of folk remedials. Sometimes they are sprinkled on, or mingled with soil, in an area of land that has been ravaged by pesti-lence. Sometimes they are put into a pillow, brushed onto the skin (like on Ash Wednesday) or mingled with wine and con-sumed. For safety purposes, only use the latter concept if the wine becomes a libation or gets used in another symbolic manner in your healing rituals.

Ashes from sacred fires were placed on or near the eyelid in Morocco, Northern Africa and in Hopi tradition to cure sore eyes. Placed on a patch of itchy skin, the Indians believe this to bring relief, while in France a similar approach is taken to swollen glands, and in Bombay application prevents headache!

Burning Emblems/Objects: Small figures formed from the clothes of an ailing person, known as a Poppet, were often stuffed with purgative herbs and ignited to symbolically purify the patient and burn away disease. However, images made from clay, paper, or wood may also be used. The configuration of this item should somehow reflect the malady (a heart for heart problems, etc.).

Candles: Carve words or emblems that reflect your wish for health half way down a candle. Anoint the candle with healing oils lightly. Burn this for seven minutes each day over 3 days, keeping the remnants for a portable amulet. Alternatively, carve the name of your sickness into the candle and stick a pin through it. Anoint the taper with banishing oil and burn it by a waning moon until the pin falls out. By this time the sickness should show signs of abating.

Fires: Passing a person over the flames of a small, well-tended fire three times is an old Scottish cure, marking the transition from sickness to health. One of the best woods for this was considered to be bramble, the thorns ensnaring the disease.

Light: Try placing a pale green or blue light bulb in the room where you spend most of your time recuperating. Keep it on both day and night, allowing the colored light's vibration to encourage the natural healing process along. These are the two colors most strongly related to health and rest in color therapy.

Pyromancy: Some healers used this ancient form of divination to determine either the course of treatment for a patient, or to know whether or not recovery was possible. For this they usually had the patient help create the fire, and observed both the building process and the flames themselves for indications.

Smoke: When an animal or person passes through the smoke of a sacred fire the smoke can carry their malady away, and grant protection. The most common example of this are the Beltane fires in Scotland, considered particularly helpful for cattle. In a modern magical circle this theme is mirrored by smudging, e.g. blessing all participants with the smoke from a sage wand.

Sunlight: In some traditions people believe that fire

cannot abide if the sun shines upon it because it was origi-
nally stolen from the sun god. Consequently, placing someone with a fever in sunlight is one folk remedial that drives
out the figurative fire within. Additionally, people suffering
from depression may benefit from getting more natural light
according to new studies.

Fire Meditation, And Visualization

For individuals who find their physical, emotional or
spiritual energy seems wanting, or those desiring drastic transformations, the element of Fire offers positive symbolism on
which to focus. The easiest type of fire to see clearly in your
mind is that of a candle flame. Or, if you have a fireplace that
you can focus on before closing your eyes, this image will work
nicely too.

Sit comfortably in front of the fire source that you wish to
envision. Begin your breathing exercises as with the other sections of this book, and release as many worries and stray
thoughts as possible. Watch the flame and make it the center of
your attention until nothing exists but its light, scent, sounds
and warmth.

When you reach this point, close your eyes and allow the
image of the flame to appear on the chalkboard of your mind.
Observe its movements; the lively dance that is fire's alone. As
this image becomes clear, slowly allow your body to appear in
the center of the flame. Have no fear, this is a spiritual fire that
also exists within you. It will bring no harm.

As the flame surrounds, sense its warmth like a blanket on a cold winter's night. Feel its energy pouring into your skin, and down to the depths of your soul. Let this energy freely flow into you until you feel you can hold no more, then begin returning to normal levels of awareness. As with the earlier exercises in this book, changing the color of the flame can help you meet specific goals in your life:

Red - Authoritative speech and actions

Yellow - Creative leadership skills

Green - Fertility (physical or mental)

Blue - Being at peace with change

Purple - Success in spiritual endeavors

An alternative to the above visualization for those desirous of modifications in their life is to begin with the visualization of a nest of flames. Think of this nest like a womb or cocoon that you will dwell in temporarily to allow metamorphosis to occur. Before embarking on this meditation, have a clear image of what transformations you wish, and truly commit yourself to them in word and deed.

In the visualization, see yourself going into the center of the nest. Here the flame becomes a sheath to your body. Within this sheath, the old is burned away and the new person is created. Take your time with this, and try to put images on the changes taking place to improve the mental effect. When the transformation is complete (or as complete as possible) emerge from the fire. See yourself like a butterfly, who now has wings to rise above the old ways and reach for the stars.

Do not be discouraged if you have to repeat this meditation regularly to engender change. Some things, like life-long habits take years to totally eradicate. Nonetheless, this exercise will help you face that necessary modification positively, giving you a tool to participate directly in making it a reality.

Rituals

Fire has numerous functions in religious ritual. In Iran, for example, there are five ritual fires. One, the Bahram, honors Ahura Mazda and is the earthly representation of the divine essence. This fire must be created from sixteen other types of fire, and must be maintained with sandalwood five times a day by a priest. Frequently the priest must ritually wash before assembling a sacred fire, or it is believed it will not light successfully.

Another example comes from India, and the worship of Agni the god who personifies fire. This god has three special ritual fires in his honor. One is in the East, called *vaisvanara*, for offerings. One is placed in the south, called *dakshia*, used for the cult of the Manes, and third is the western fire called *garhapatya*, for cooking.

Some of Fire's significance in ritual comes from its by-products; smoke and ashes. Smoke was equated to the prayers of the faithful by the early Hebrews, Christians and the American Indians alike. While ancient people turned to resinous gums for aromatic praises, the American Indians burned tobacco on their sacred fire as both a prayer and an offering.

Ashes seemed to carry the same purgative quality as the fire itself, without the painful heat. In India, purgatory ash baths precede ritual. Brahmans rub themselves with ashes to prepare for religious ceremonies. Hindus take the ashes from fires honoring Darma Rajah and use them to drive away malevolent spirits. Aztec priests blacked their faces before religious rites, and in Hebrew tradition ashes from an offering were mixed with water to expel defilement that comes from contact with a corpse.

In modern magical circles, fire plays an important role in honoring the sun's movement across the sky and for purifying rites. Emblems for fire are traditionally placed in the southern quarter, most often a candle. Frequently, symbolic items are given to ritual fires to release a spell or aid in banishing spirits or other negative energies. For example, someone who is quitting smoking might offer their pack of cigarettes to a spring fire to externally mark the change occurring within. Similarly, during some late summer festivals it is traditional to toss one's braided crown of corn into the fires to receive a wish.

Spellcraft

In adding fire as a component to your spells, remember that you can do so by adding heat, sunlight (or other light sources), or by using flame itself and its by-product ashes.

Ashes: Besides their use in healing, ashes from sacred

fires became an integral component to numerous spells including those to fertilize fields, divine information, weather magic, and banishing negativity. In most cases the ashes were either sprinkled on a surface or mixed with another substance for application.

For weather magic specifically, ashes thrown in the air bring fair weather in Spain, to disperse mist in Peru, clear a cloudy sky in Brazil, and to calm a wind in South America. The Bohemians scatter ashes in their fields to prevent hailstorms. A similar custom exists in France where this action acts to ward against thunder and lightning strikes.

To improve fertility or abundance, ashes got scattered over wanting fields. This also insured the fecundity of flocks and a plentiful milk supply in ancient Rome. Ashes from an Easter fire specifically, or those of the Midsummer fire (Germany, Ireland) were fed to animals for similar purposes.

Igniting with a Fire: Burning a symbolic object, or paper which details one's needs, is a very old magical practice that is marvelously simple and effective. Please make certain to have a fire-proof container in which to burn things, and do not leave them unattended while they are consumed. Afterwards, the ashes can be scattered to disperse the energy, or carried as an amulet.

Light: Because of the positive symbolism light evokes, it is a very effective tool for spells, especially the use of a common light bulb. Find an aromatic oil that represents your goal, dab a bit on your bulbs and then when you turn on the bulb the heat and light release both energy and scent to fulfill your magic!

Warming by a Fire: The warmth that fire produces is another good emblem, especially in matters of the heart. Say, for example, you've had a fight with someone. You could place their portrait near a warm area (the heater if you don't have a hearth) to help figuratively "warm up" that situation.

Holiday Observances

The two major objects in humankind's sky—the moon and the sun—became central to many holiday observances. An awareness of the sun's movement through the sky, and the growth and shortening of days, were very important to survival. By having specific festivals that marked that movement, common people could be more aware of when best to sow their crops, harvest, and travel abroad.

In general, Fire festivals often honored the sun in some way. They either rejoiced in its life-giving energy in the spring and summer, or tried to support and energize its return to power throughout the winter.

1/11 Burning of the Clavie: Fishermen in Scotland place barrels on poles, ignite them then walk all the streets in town. The ashes get collected by watchers for charms.

1/14 Carnival at Oudenberg: Belgian festival where

one tree is burned each year as remnants of Druidic rites that honor the sun god.

1/25 St. Paul's Day: If it's sunny today, it portends a happy year.

2/2 Candlemas: Today, white candles are lit to chase away the shadows in our lives and give strength to the sun in its journey.

2/20 Installation of the new Lama: Old Tibetan festival which took place every three years, part of which includes ritual fires made with salt, wine and sulphur to carry away the evils of the past years.

2/26 Mihr Fires: Armenian fire festival for prosperity and a bountiful harvest.

3/9 Tibetan Butter Festival: Part of this celebration includes divination by the flame from butter lamps, which is observed carefully for insights.

3/13 Balinese Purification Feast: This celebration includes one special altar set up to honor the sun.

3/16 Spring Fire Festival: Also called the Holi in Bengal.

Late March/Early April Easter: Folk tales claim the sun dances for joy this day, and any who cannot see it are being blocked by the devil.

4/16 Spring Festival: Zurich celebration where a cotton figurine is burned to bring fertility and blessings.

4/18 Rama's Day: Indian festival honoring the 4th incarnation of Vishnu, the sun god, who represented chivalry, honor and strength.

4/22: St. George's Eve: In many parts of Europe St. George is a solar figure who chases evil from the land, at least metaphorically.

4/30 Walpurgis Night: Bun Rosemary, juniper and sloe to banish blight and mildew from crops.

Ash Wednesday: The first day of lent and a time when penitence is marked with sacred ashes. In some regions, people also anoint doorways with ashes to mark a time of quite introspection.

5/1 Beltane: A fire and fertility festival that marks the return of life to the earth with boisterous rituals and revelry.

5/19 Kallyntaria & Plynteria: Greek festival of purification, akin to spring cleaning.

Festival of Pure Brightness: 22nd of 6th moon (China): Spring festival of a very elaborate nature including the ceremonial rekindling of fires in the Imperial Palace. Afterwards processions continue as do prayers and celebration.

Month of June - Festival of the Sun: Incan celebration where the sun is commemorated with offerings of tea and rice, along with dance and song at sunrise and sunset.

6/8 Dragon Boat Festival: Chinese celebration that mimics the yearly struggle between light and darkness.

6/21 Summer Solstice: Earth is now half way around the sun in its travels and this is the longest period of light during the year. Fairies love this holiday. It is also a time for harvesting magical herbs now saturated with solar energy.

8/1 Lammas: Harvest festival during which Scottish

people toss a corn husk crown into the ritual fires with a wish.

8/11 Perseid Meteor Shower: During this period the sky is alive with fire, giving us pause to contemplate the fires of spirit within and without.

Early Sept. Apache Sunrise Ceremony: An initiatory rite for young women into adulthood which begins with the first signs of dawn, marking not only a new day but a new life and role in the community.

Mid Sept. Summer's End: A fire festival for good health and protection from the coming cold of fall and winter.

9/20 Birthday of the Sun: China.

9/22 Fall Equinox: The date when darkness and light share the sky equally. Egyptians tried to help the sun maintain its power during their observations of his holiday by holding staves to the sky for support.

Mid October Floating of the Lamps: Thailand's festival to celebrate the awakening of, and insight given to, humankind's spirit.

10/31 Samhain: This ancient word for the festival which has become known as Halloween means "fires of peace." The Druids settled all quarrels of their region around the ritual fires tonight.

11/8 Festival of the Kitchen Goddess: Today the Japanese honor the goddess of the hearth and all domestic fires, which provide food.

11/16 Diwali: Hindu celebration of the New year during which lights, candles and gold colored items are set out to draw prosperity into people's lives, and drive away any evil spirits that may linger about.

Late November Tibetan Festival of Lights: This commemorates the ascension of one of the Lamas, founders with a plethora of illumination, symbolizing the awakening soul.

12/8 Birthday of Amaterasu: Celebrating the Japanese goddess of the sun.

Working With Fire Devas

Without material fire, Fire devas called salamanders cannot exist. Likewise, no spark to begin any fire can be created without their assistance. The term salamander comes from a word meaning hearth or fire place. As one might expect, these beings live in any type of energy spark or flame, including electrical ones. Sometimes, however, salamanders use the medium of smoke from incense or a fire to assist in manifesting themselves.

The salamander's size is directly dependent on the size of the energy source in which they abide. Medieval writers depicted the smaller class as lizardlike and about one foot long. Larger salamanders appear as robed in fiery armor, rather like the fire genie (the effrete) of Arabic lore.

Among this class of deva the Acthnici were some of the most important, appearing as a distinct globe, which we sometimes call St. Elmo's Fire, the Hermit's Lantern and/or Will-o-the-Wisp. Salamanders are also considered the strongest of the elementals. Yet despite their power, many ancient mages kept their distance, feeling that the study of salamanders was not always worth the risk of literally "playing with fire."

People with tons of energy and fervor will attract salamanders naturally. These are the individuals to whom you can turn, even in drizzly weather, to get a good fire going! Within the human body, this deva evidences itself in the emotional nature and through body heat. Without the salamanders, there would be no warmth in a hug, or in our words!

This deva teaches us to live fully every moment. They know that when the flames die, so do they. Consequently, salamanders are always depicted as happy and dancing the jig of life. Nonetheless, this representation is not complete. Salamanders tend toward strong emotions, sometimes the negative ones like anger, exuberance, and impatience because of the short time they have. In working with the other elementals, Air devas excite Fire, Earth devas control and contain it, and Water devas create smoke but also tend to extinguish the flame. Please bear this in mind in your requests to this deva.

Appropriate behests for the salamanders include:

• Renewing or improving the warmth and joy of a friendship

•Exposing hidden or secret matters

• Improving personal energy, especially for a specific project

• Banishing negative thought forms and habits

• Lighting the way for personal change, or transformation of relationships

- Energizing the passionate self
- Generating better self images and more confidence
- Instilling strength to handle a difficult authoritative position
- Victory over trying circumstances or dark moods
- Growing comprehension (e.g. the proverbial light bulb going on)

Fire Spirits

As is evident throughout this chapter, working with the Fire spirits should be a well considered endeavor. Know well the risks you face ahead of time, and prepare yourself by learning to work with the other elements effectively first. Remember that even shamans consider Fire a potent, but sometimes dangerous, magical companion.

Big Heads: Iroquois stone giants whose eyes are flame. These spirits fly among the storms supported by their hair.

Chou Yang: Chinese emperor who taught people how to use fire to drive away snakes and wild animals, to keep enemies at bay, and for smithing.

Garuda: Hindu form of the sun and vehicle for Vishnu, the Garuda is represented as half man, half bird with a golden body and fire-red wings. As the fatal enemy of all snakes, one who suffers from a snake bite may find a cure by hugging a pillar at one of Garuda's temples.

Hob: English house fairy who lives near and protects the heart. Welcome this spirit with sweet cream left near the stove.

Huo Sheng: Chinese magical priest who changed himself into a giant during one of the battles of the Chou Dynasty. His main ability was that of throwing flames on the enemy.

Logi: Teutonic giant whose name meant, and dominion was, the wild fire.

Penates: Roman spirits who guard the hearth fires.

Shawnodese: Native American Spirit Keeper of the south.

Sudhri: Norse dwarf who rules over the southern quarter of creation and fire.

Surtr: The Norse giant with a flaming sword which is the instrument of the apocalypse.

Will-o-the-wisp: A mysterious hovering, round flame also known as fox fire, friar's lantern and corpse lights. This supernatural manifestation has different characteristics in various cultures. In Germany it is a wandering or lost soul. The Wends believe it to be the spirit of an unbaptized baby. American Indians believed it to be a fire creature that presaged calamity,

> **Without material fire, Fire devas called salamanders, cannot exist.**

and in Africa the fiery balls represent witches sent to terrify wrong-doers.

Yama & Vamana: Hindu guardian of the south and its protective elephant who supports that quarter of creation, respectively.

Zaltys: Green spirit-snake who the sun goddess adored. One type, the Aitvares, gave off light and could fly.

Fire Deities

Fire deities are not as difficult to work with as Fire spirits because most of these figures have other attributes than simply the Fire element upon which to focus and call. Do, however, remember their flaming nature in your magical workings. The fires of assistance, of knowledge, of power usually bear a price.

Agni: Hindu demon slayer and fire god whose emblems include the axe, torch, fan and the color red.

Amida: Japanese buddha of infinite light and protector of humankind. In Tibet: Amitabha.

Anala: Hindu divine being who personifies fire and attends Indra.

Apollo: Roman god whose name means "shining". Presides over law and justice. Burn bay leaf as incense.

Aryaman: India; god of the sun and all heavenly gifts.

Atar: Persian god who personifies the Fire element,, and brings comfort, virility and love to humankind. For those who are virtuous, Atar promises paradise. Only vegetarian meals are suitable to this divine being, to whom cooked dead flesh is an insult.

Atmu: Egyptian aspect of the sun god in the evening. Also called Atum, Tem or Tum, this was a self created deity. His imagery is that of an elderly man bearing the double crown of Upper and Lower Egypt upon his head.

Atnatu: Australian Kaitish for the god who created himself, then rose to the sky becoming the father and benefactor of humankind.

Balder: Aesir bright sun god, and god of happiness. Offer him libations of well water.

Bel: Irish sun god whose name means "shining." His festival is Beltane.

Bran the Blessed: Welsh prophetic sun god. His sacred animals are ravens.

Byelobog: Slavonic god of light and day. His color is white.

Chu-jung: Chinese god of fire and revenge.

Dazhbog: Slavonic mighty god who conquers the shadows and presides over any decision for equity.

Dhata: In India, a creator god who embodies beneficent fires.

Durago: Philippine goddess of the Volcano.

Durga: Hindu goddess of protection who equates to St. George. Her emblems are the lion, drum, and sword.

Frey: Vanir sun god presiding over passion, fertility, wealth, oaths and sunshine. His animals are the horse and boar.

Gibil: Babylonian god of fire.

Gordniu: Irish/Welsh smithy god who forged the Tuatha's weapons. Offer him libations of any brewed beverages.

Indra: Solar lord of the gods in India who embodies destructive fires including lightning. Also the god of bravery and reincarnation. Honor him with libations of any wine made from plants.

Jupiter: Roman god of light who also controls matters of justice and wealth.

Lugh: Irish/Welsh Fair One, god of sun and battle. Sacred animals are the raven and white stag.

Mahui-kie: Polynesian fire goddess and goddess of the volcano.

Nasatyas: Twin Indian gods of morning who protect love and marriage. Sacred animals are birds and horses.

Ogma: Irish sun-faced god who invented writing. Honor him with invocations of poetry.

Parjanya: Indian cloud dweller whose warm solar rays bathe the earth.

Pele: Hawaiian goddess of volcanic fire from whom one does not take a souvenir without propitiation. Hula dance is sacred to her.

Peron: Slavonic god of fire similar to Jupiter or Thor in depiction. His sacred tree is the oak.

Rock-sens: Gambian creator of lightning. Appease him with rain water.

Rugaba: Ugandan sun god and creator whose colors are sky blue and yellow.

Savitri: India; morning and evening aspects of the sun and dispeller of problems.

Shamash: Babylonian sun god whose light is the hand of justice. Sacred emblems for this god are the scepter and ring.

Surya: India; chief solar deity and god of enlightenment. Colors are dark red and copper.

Svarog: Slavonic bright god of clear skies. His colors are white and gold. Leave metals on your altar for him.

Thor: Norse god of thunder, lightning, strength, and defense.

Tien mu: Chinese god of lightning.

Uma: India; goddess of light, fertility and a mediator between humans and the divine. Worship her in high places, especially mountain tops.

Ushas: The god of dawn who brings wellbeing and vitality to all things. Her sacred animals are horses.

Varuna: India; sun god and god of law, creator and judge. Libations of water are suitable to him.

Vesta: Roman goddess of the hearth and the ever-burning sacred fires. Her sacred animals include the goat and donkey. Her festival date is June 7.

Vishnu: India; god whose light permeates the universe. Sacred emblems include the lotus, a conch shell and the serpent.

Vulcan: Roman god of fire and the forge. His festival dates are 8/17, 8/23, and 8/27. Sacred symbols include a hammer and thunderbolt. Offer him minerals.

Walo: Australian goddess of the sun.

Wayland: Germanic Lord of smiths and prince to the fairy folk. His animal is the horse. Offer him metals.

Zorya: Slavonic goddess of the morning star who tended the sun's horses.

Correspondence List

ANIMALS & INSECTS: Desert dwelling creatures, those with stingers or whose bite is poisonous. Many mammals (warm blooded). Asp, cricket, dragonfly (also air), firedrake (Germanic/Celtic), fire ants, iguana, kestrel, lion, lizard, mantis, mosquito, mouse (Native American), porcupine, prairie dogs, rattle snake, scorpion.

APPLICATIONS: Authority, achievement, banishing, blessing, cleansing, drastic change, energizing, enlightenment, expansion, friendship, happiness, knowledge, leadership, legal matters, light, passion, purification, reincarnation, self actualization and assurance, sexuality and fertility, success, truth.

ARCHANGEL: Michael or Ariel.

ASTROLOGICAL SIGNS: Aries, Leo, Sagittarius.

CELESTIAL INFLUENCES: The Sun, Mars, Jupiter.

COLOR: White (Enochian), yellow (Mayan, Mexican, Cheyenne), vermillion and red (China, Native American, Zuni), blue (Navaho). Also used metaphysically: vibrant orange and gold.

CRYSTALS, MINERALS, STONES: Agates (banded, red), amber, apache tear, asbestos, bloodstone, brass, carnelian, citrine, diamond (including Herkimer), fire opal, flint, garnet, gold, hematite, iron, jasper (red), lava, meteorite, pyrite, serpentine, spinel, steel, sulphur, sunstone, tiger's eye, topaz, tourmaline (red), zircon.

DIRECTION Traditionally south. North (Mexico).

EMBLEMS: Bonfire, brazier, candles, censer, incense burner, lantern, lightning, red objects, sun, stars.

FOOD ITEMS (MISC): Alcohol, barbecued foods, beer, cashew, cocoa, coffee, honey, horseradish, mustard, olive (also air), pretzel, salsa, sunflower seeds, tea, tortilla, vinegar, walnut, wine. Any flaming or very spicy style of food such as Szechuan.

FRUITS & VEGETABLES: Artichoke, carambola, carrot, celery, chili, chives, citron, corn, fig, leek, lime, mango, nettles, onion (also earth), orange, peppers (red), pineapple, pomegranate, prickly pear, radish (also earth), raisin, shallot, sloe berries, squash, tangerine, watercress (also water). Most citrus fruits.

One of the most important lessons of Fire lay in its light.

GENDER: Masculine.

GREEK SHAPE: Tetrahedral.

HEBRAIC QUARTER: Yamin (also meaning "right").

HERBS: Allspice, angelica, basil, bay, chamomile, cinnamon, clove, copal, coriander, cumin, curry, damiana, dill, fennel, frankincense, garlic, ginger, ginseng, golden seal, grains of paradise, heliotrope, lovage, mandrake, mullein, mustard, nutmeg, olibanum, pennyroyal, pepper, peppermint, rosemary, rue, saffron, sarsaparilla, sassafras, sesame.

LOCATIONS: The desert, any dry or arid spot of soil, volcanoes, near bonfires or explosions, hot springs and saunas (also water).

MOON PHASE: Full.

MOONS (Folk Names): Cactus Blossom Moon (March), Ashes Moon (April), Hot Moon (June), Sun House Moon (July), Red Moon (August), Blood Moon (October), Gold Moon and Ashes Fire Moon (December).

PLANTS, TREES, FLOWERS: Alder, almond (flowering), anemone, ash, avens, bloodroot, cactus, carnation, cattail, cedar, flax, gorse, hawthorn, hibiscus, hickory, holly, horse chestnut, juniper, larch, mahogany, marigold, oak, poppy (red), prickly ash, rowan, snap dragon, sumac, sunflower, thistle, tobacco, walnut, witch hazel, woodruff, wormwood.

SEASON: Summer.

SENSE: Sight.

TATTWAS SYMBOL (INDIA): Tijas—a red triangle.

TAROT EMBLEMS: Swords, daggers (other man-made weapons). Also the Sun card; The Tower, brought down by lightning; Death for its drastic transformative power and the Emperor who is a solar god.

TIME: Noon; Sunday.

WIND (Name): Notus (the South wind).

"Spirit" by Colleen Koziara

We turn to spirit for help
when our foundations are shaking
only to find out
it is the spirit shaking us.
— The Peaceful Warrior

Chapter Seven
Spirit–source–ether– the Void

I washed my face in water, that neither rained
nor run; I dried my face on a towel, that was neither
wove nor spun.'
— Old Riddle whose answer is "dew and sun."

f all chapters in this book, this one might rightfully be the largest, but ultimately it became the smallest. At one point I seriously considered just leaving a blank or mirrored page as the entirety of text. Why? Because the way Spirit is perceived by each individual is very personal and distinct. If you asked ten different people of the same religious background to describe or paint their image of Spirit, each depiction would contain unique facets that directly reflect individual vision.

I have never believed that one should try and put "god in a box." When you define something you also limit it. Spirit, be it human, divine or elemental, has no limits or boundaries, nor will I try to create any herein. Instead, this chapter will discuss the element of spirit as represented religiously, mythologically and philosophically. From this vantage point, I leave it up to your own sensibilities to determine what vision you have of Spirit, and what that means in your reality, specifically in your elemental encounters.

In talking of Spirit throughout this chapter, we are actually touching on several different constructs. First is the human construct of the soul.

As the carrier of past-life memories, and the essential spark of individuality, the soul is part of Spirit, and dramatically affected by this element. How can it not be? All children are affected by their parent in some way, often seeking to emulate, or return to oneness with, that parent. In some instances, as will be seen in the next section of this chapter, the two almost seem synonymous because of this intimate connection.

Secondly, we are talking of the Great Spirit whose spark abides within all things. This spark gave birth to creation, and continues to manifest in many wonders within the human ingenuity. Additionally, the energy of the Great Spirit maintains life, provides continuance and coherence, and reminds us that we are all connected, if only remotely, to one greater good.

Finally, and perhaps most importantly for this book, we are speaking of the element of Spirit which binds all other elements together into a functional system. This aspect of spirit acts as an invisible, mysterious guide and glue for the fabric of the Universe. Some might call this entity kismet, others karma, others still Fate, but whatever its name the other elementals could not exist or work together without Spirit's direct intercession. Thus, while spirit is the fifth point of the pentagram, it is also the center of the square which unites, upholds and supports all of creation.

Myths And Legends

The Spirit of nature became a central theme in Native American traditions. Apache Indians call these beings *hactcin*, each of which personifies objects and forces in the Earth and Sky. These potent forces compare with the Pueblo and Hopi depiction of kachinas, all of whom are honored in sacred dances. It is also among the Native Americans that we hear the term Great Spirit as referring to the creative force behind all life.

The Great Spirit has many names including Master of Life, Father Sky, the Arch of Heaven and the Great Mystery. Out of reverence toward such great power, the Sioux choose not to depict it in definite form but through symbols. In this, and many other plain Indian traditions, the other spirits of earth, air, fire and water (e.g. the deva) intermediate between the Great Spirit and humankind.

Among Hindus, the vital essence of one's soul is called

atman. This is also the spiritual essence of the world. It embodies life, form, light, space, is all-comprehensive and self existent, much like the Great Spirit. In this ideology, the soul is psychical, and wholly linked with the greater life-force of the planet.

Polynesian beliefs discuss *mana* as a mysterious spiritual power that saturates the universe and all that dwells therein, including inanimate objects.

Egyptians called the essence of humankind's soul the *ba*.

Mana underlies all life, and is wholly good except when put to evil ends. At times, *mana* has physical manifestation, but it operates on a higher order. For example, a fisherman who receives a good catch believes there is *mana* in his net. Thus, the virtues of *mana* are potent, but it seems unable to operate independent of creation.

In Guiana there is an interesting term for spirit, *winti*, which also means "wind." This was chosen because, like the wind, supernatural beings do not have material substance. Additionally, the practitioners of magic here take the name *winti-man* indicating their strong connection with the spiritual world.

Among the Jains, the soul or life principle within all matter is called *jiva*. *Jiva* cannot be quantified, it is indestructible, ever-forming and ever working within the material plane. If the Jain live their life correctly the *jiva* within them is liberated into a self aware space, free of the material world.

Egyptians called the essence of humankind's soul the *ba*. This *ba* inhabited the body during life, left at death, and would eventually return to the body again. Consequently, the living relatives would often leave cakes, wines and finery in Egyptian tombs so that the body would have nourishment and life's pleasures when the *ba*, sometimes characterized as a bird with a lamp, finally returned from its resting place; the stars.

The Egyptian and Jain beliefs surrounding death and the soul also illustrate another nearly universal concept; the existence of a specific place or plane in which spirits dwell. Some call this Paradise, Nirvana, the Land of the Grandfather, Heaven and even Purgatory, but no matter the name the idea is strikingly similar. After death, the life essence returns to the All, to a place of rest, or to a waiting ground in which it will dwell forever or find rebirth. In either case, the spark of individuality is never truly lost. It, like all energy, simply changes form.

Folklore, Superstition, Magick

In terms of folklore for the element of Spirit, by far the most predominant beliefs surround the human soul after death, and especially ghosts and apparitions.

Contacting & Seeing Spirits

• On Halloween in Mexico parents of children who died in the last year leave marigolds and firecrackers on their walkway believing the child's spirit can follow these home and visit for the holiday.

• It is easiest to see spirits on New Years at Midnight because this is when the Veil between the Worlds grows thin. Other dates associated with this phenomena include 8/1 (Lammas) and 10/31 (Hallows).

• According to Scottish tradition, go to a graveyard at midnight. There you will see the soul of the last person buried guarding the cemetery.

• When trying to contact a spirit through a seance, it is helpful to have a personal item that belonged to that soul. This will help draw the spirit back to reclaim that item.

• A child born on Friday at 12 p.m. can see both ghosts and the fairies. The same holds true for the 7th son of the 7th son, whereas a child born on Christmas will never see a spirit.

Displeased Spirits

• Many early societies regarded earthquakes and volcano eruptions (or other natural disasters) as an indication that the gods were displeased and needed an offering.

• If you've encountered an angry spirit, check its burial shroud. If there are any knots in this, they must be undone or the spirit cannot move on to the next life.

Presence of Spirits

• A bird, snail or hare that suddenly appears in a place in which it would normally not be is often the spirit of a person who has just passed over. The animal helps the spirit move from one life to the next, or in some belief systems may actually be an incarnation.

• A candle flame burning blue reveals the presence of a spirit.

Protection from Spirits

• If you feel the need to protect your home from spirits, hang a mirror on a window or door facing outward to reflect them back to their proper resting place.

• St. John's Wort, fennel and/or salt are all effective agents for protecting oneself or home from the presence of unwanted spirits.

• Folk custom claims that evil spirits and mischievous fairies alike are afraid of the color red, because it is the color of life.

• To keep a spirit from wandering, the body should be buried feet first.

• A first-born child has no need for fairy and spirit protection. According to lore they are blessed with natural wards against all such encounters.

• To turn a ghost or other entity out of your home, turn the door around so it faces the other way. Similarly, after someone's death, rearrange all the furniture in the home so if the spirit returns they won't recognize the house, and leave.

• Carrying a four leaf clover will allow you to see a spirit's or fairies' deceptions.

• The ringing of church bells drives away malevolent spirits.

• Burning elder, hanging holly or carrying iron are all effective safeguards against wandering ghosts.

Attunement

Spirit is a catalyst that blends all the other elements together in harmony, including you as one component of the equation. You have spirit; the world has spirit; the energy of life is Spirit. Therefore, attuning to Spirit requires an intimate exploration of self as a part of the greater picture.

Such explorations are very personal, akin to a quest where the driving goal is self awareness and reunion with the Sacred. Consequently, I cannot give precise directions on how to achieve this aim. There are some steps that may help, however.

First, take some time alone. Fast for three days if it is physically feasible, and spend time in direct contact with things that represent all four elements. One good place is a beach at sunrise and sunset, where the sun's fire, the water, the sand (earth/fire) and wind all combine to create a special ambiance very suitable to inner-journeys (see Meditation).

Next, in preparing for your adventure, bring along your journal and any other personal religious symbols that will help you totally focus on Spirit, and the Spirit in you. A portable tape player with quiet music may help, but the simple sounds of nature also have potential here—they too can be a teacher and guide.

Most importantly, don't begin your attunement period with any expectations of what may, or may not, happen. You will likely not experience flashing lights or visitations. Ultimately, Spirit speaks to us with the "Still Small Voice" deep in our hearts or through the subtle messages from Earth. Don't be afraid to ask the devas of your location to help in this quest. That is one behest suitable to any elemental!

Know too that attuning to, and an understanding of Spirit is a life-long endeavor. It will not stop after your initial attempt. From that day forward your life becomes a ritual wherein the Spirit of All is sought, honored and integrated.

Exactly what Spirit teaches you will depend much on what you need to grow. There are some universal lessons of spirit, however. They include learning to perceive life from a higher perspective and accepting all living things as part of a great network (and treating them accordingly). Spirit also guides us toward more light-filled ideas and ways of living, so that in the next existence we can move closer to oneness.

Spirit Healing

Spirit healing may be looked at in one of two ways. The first is what we call faith healing where the power of the Sacred is channeled into a person to effect a cure, often via the laying on of hands. In this instance the healer is nothing more than a circuit, directing and guiding the energy given by Spirit to where it is most needed. Many healers who work in this field also say they feel Spirit guiding and directing where their hands should go for the most direct flow.

The second form of Spirit Healing is any technique

that blends two or more elements together for improved, multidimensional effects. For example, in the 1500s Dr. Sigismund Bacstrom wrote that if all the elements could be blended into one stone, that stone could heal any malady. He represented this miraculous curative by two interlaced triangles—the Star of David—which has been used throughout the ages as a protective talisman.

For the purpose of this chapter, I am going to focus on mingling elements together using Spirit as the glue of cohesiveness. We know from observing nature that the elements rarely work alone; they cooperate. In healing, learning to use this cooperation should improve the results, if only on a spiritual level. Here are some examples:

Ash (Earth/Fire): For this symbolism use only ashes that come from the burning of wood. To add more elemental symbolism, choose a specifically aligned tree, or blend in some herbs that correspond to your needs. Apply this only externally, and keep it away from potential areas of infection.

Incense (Air/Fire): Because it burns, incense is associated with Fire, but its aroma is carried by Air. Additionally, the scent represented could be any of the four elements to increase the effect. For example: burning Patchouli incense corrosponds to earth + air + fire.

Mud or Wet Clay (Earth/Water): A time-honored

beauty technique, bury your malady in the mud or clay. When it hardens, that strong surface protects you against the negative energies. For more symbolism, use red clay to add a Fire element or a yellow clay for Air.

Sand (Fire/Earth/Water): Depending on where one gathers this component, minimally two, and possibly all three elements come into play. Desert sand has a strong Fire element whereas beach sand has a far more potent Water element. Once gathered sand can be tossed to the winds with a malady, returned to the earth, placed in a healing brazier to disburse heat, etc.

> **Exactly what Spirit teaches you will depend much on what you need to grow.**

Seaside Winds (Water & Air): At sundown, place two chairs a small space apart from each other with the backs facing. Lay a cloth over each back so it is stretched slightly inbetween. In the morning squeeze out the resulting dew, carried on the wind and waves of the ocean. The resulting liquid can be used in a tincture or an anointing water. Because of the salt content, this preparation also has an underlying earth element to draw upon for extra cleansing.

Steam (Fire/Water/Air): An excellent aid to colds and allergy attacks, the only caution here is that one doesn't get burnt on the hot water. The best solution for this is standing in the bathroom while a hot shower runs. To add in more elemental symbolism, place a cache of symbolic herbs under the water to release their scent like aromatherapy!

Meditation, Spirit And Visualization

For individuals who feel out of touch with the Sacred or their own soul, Spirit is a good place to begin but also one of the most elusive having no real form except that which our imagination can provide. If you have a specific divinity upon whom you call regularly, having a picture of that persona might help this exercise.

For Spirit meditations I suggest lying down for two reasons. First, any encounter with Spirit can be somewhat overwhelming physically. Many individuals report feeling dizzy or close to swooning because of the enormity of power and vastness that Spirit embodies. Secondly, from a historical precedence, should you fall asleep during this meditation, dreams are another way for the divine to speak to your heart. Here, the mind is freer to accept messages from the Super Conscious, the Universe, or Spirit.

Begin as you did with the other meditations in this book, breathing in an all-connected relaxed manner. Let the pace of life naturally slow down. There is no need to rush here, no worries, no duties, just you and Spirit.

As you feel your body becoming weightless and relaxed, begin envisioning a bright, silvery-white light pouring down upon you from overhead. The center of this light is so bright and pure you almost can't look directly at it. It is warm and welcoming, and seems very familiar to you. At this juncture some people find it helpful to put a face in the center of the light, namely that of their guiding god or goddess. This is perfectly fine to help establish a personal connection. However, be mindful that this chosen image is but one facet, one representation, of something far greater and larger than we can comprehend as mortals.

When the image of the light is clear and crisp, reach your hands upward to welcome it. Speak to the light, ask for its aid in knowing both Spirit and yourself better, then embrace its energy. Let the light saturate your pores, your blood, your very cells. Know it as part of your being.

Commune here as long as you feel the need. Spirit has no time constraints. It is infinite in patience and power and will stay with you until you feel whole. Even after the visualization, know that Spirit's presence never really leaves you. It's form only changes to something you carry in your heart, mind and soul.

Unlike the other elemental meditations, I do not recommend changing the color of this light to correspond with specific needs. White is a color that represents the purest, undefiled energy with which you wish to connect. Consequently, it has as infinite an application in your meditations as does Spirit itself.

An alternative meditation that helps connect with one's internal Spirit begins similarly. Only this time, picture your heart chakra as having a flame in the center. If you look closely this flame forms an infinity sign, a DNA helix, or something else that you personally identify with the immutable soul. When the image is com-

> **Once one is touched by Spirit, they will never be the same.**

pletely three-dimensional, allow it to grow until that picture overlaps your entire body.

Now have the overlay and your physical being merge visually, the symbol sinking slowly into your skin. Feel its familiarity, its comforting presence, the way its energy awakens each chakra. Once the emblem has totally soaked in, it will naturally return to the original size and location at your heart, for this is where it always resides.

Make notes of any sensations or emotions you felt during this exercise as they will be very helpful in coming to know Spirit within and without better.

Rituals

Religious ritual by its nature evokes and honors Spirit. That is its purpose. Exactly what occurred in ritual to help draw that presence, however, changed depending on the ceremony, culture and time period one examines. Beyond the use of meditation to reach a deep, altered state of awareness as discussed earlier this chapter, ancient peoples found many ways to reach out to, and unite themselves with, the Source.

One way was through sacred dance. Here the act of dancing mimics the movements of the universe to, again, encourage a heightened awareness. Once the music, rhythm and movement created a trance state, the dancer could become "possessed" by Spirit, and communicate its wishes. The most potent surviving example of this is the Whirling Dervishes who prophecize after ecstatic dance.

Another way of communing with Spirit came through the use of drums. Here, sound becomes a guide to the Shaman or seeker to follow to the gates of Spirit within themselves. The pace of the drumming is often slow and steady, sometimes increasing at the height of the experience.

Some civilizations, such as that of ancient Greece and Persia, turned to natural hallucinogenic substances to originate the trance state for ritual. It should be noted however, that this was not a recreational "trip." Such substances were regarded as sacred. Anyone found abusing them would pay dearly for such an offense to, and misuse of, Spirit, sometimes with their lives. In Persia, specifically, even the harvesting of plants for making Soma, the trance-inducing beverage, was a holy ritual performed with preciseness.

Beyond these examples, the movements, words and actions of sacred rituals are designed specifically to help engender an atmosphere within the ritual space that welcomes Spirit's participation. Each facet also prepares the participant for Spirit's presence, so that they can best benefit from the visitation. The way each person feels this presence is quite personal, but those who have will not likely forget it. Once one is touched by Spirit, they will never be the same.

Spells

In spellcraft, Spirit is the binding tie to more than one element. It also can become the driving force and guidance for the magic you create. The best way to achieve this is by calling on Spirit for aid and/or blessings. This can be done in a "generic" form using the less specific designations of Great Spirit, the One, the All, or something similar. Or, you may use the name of a specific god or goddess as a focal point for Spirit's intervention.

If you do choose to call on a divine visage to aid your elemental spells, please turn to those with whom you are most familiar *first*, properly honoring that being in your Sacred Space somehow. While the name of this Being is but a symbol for something greater, names have power and characteristics. Calling upon an unfamiliar deity, therefore, may not engender the results you wish because of those inherent characteristics.

Since we are mortal, with limited spiritual vision due to that mortality, allowing Spirit to guide and direct our magic has many benefits. For one, it can help deter unanticipated negative outcomes simply because we didn't have an infinite, universal

216

outlook with which to work. Secondly, if a spell was miscast accidentally, Spirit can step in and correct errors in the resulting energy signatures. Finally, Spirit has unlimited power with which to help manifest your magic.

Despite these advantages, I do not suggest calling on Spirit unless you are sure of your motives and are willing to follow up on a mundane level to help see your magic fulfilled. As a slight variation on an old saying, "Spirit helps those who help themselves." In other words we have to be ready, willing and able to meet Spirit half way with energy and effort of our own. Such efforts are more than worthwhile however, as when human spirit and divine spirit intersect, not only magic but miracles can happen.

Holiday Observances

For this section I have chosen holidays that return our minds and hearts to our Spiritual nature in some manner, or those that honor all elements equally in their celebrations. Besides these, any traditional festival that remembers a facet of the Divine by specific names and attributes is a suitable time to redirect your focus toward Spirit and its workings.

2/29 Leap Year: A very magical day since it happens only once every four years (one year per element).

March 22 - Spring Equinox: Ghanian New Year during which shrines are cleansed so that the new year may begin without spiritual blemish. This is also when an ancient

Babylonian festival took place commemorating the marriage of heaven and earth.

Late March - Passover: Jewish festival celebrating spiritual freedom, specifically from the hands of cruel overlords in Egypt.

3/25 - Hilaria: Roman festival where laughter is prescribed as the best medicine for body, mind and Spirit.

4/8 Birthday of Buddha: A Chinese and Japanese festival which emulates the path toward enlightenment and oneness with Spirit.

Early Summer Alaskan Whale Dance: A time when people honor the spirits of creatures who provide food.

Late July - Kachina Dances: Hopi festival that revels in the tribe's protecting, guiding spirits (e.g. the Kachinas).

8/1 Lammas: A European harvest festival during which time both fairies and spirits are thought to visit the human realm.

8/1-8/3 Day of the Dryads: Macedonian celebration during which the elemental demi-gods are honored.

9/13 All Soul's Day: Egyptian festival very similar to Hallows in its veneration of ancestral spirits.

10/1 Festival of the Dead: Chinese rite designed to protect spirits from cold or hunger in the afterlife.

Late Autumn - Feast of Lamps & Lights: Brazilian and Chinese holidays that celebrate Spirit, hope and the human quest for perfection.

10/2 - Feast of the Guardian Angel: Spanish observance giving thanks to the Spirits who guide and protect us.

10/31 Halloween: Another commemorative occasion for the dead, in Mexico parents of dead children leave out marigolds and firecrackers so the child's spirit may visit this night. In Europe, this is another date during which the veil between worlds grows thin, being the Celtic New Year.

11/1 - Lunanthishees: Irish observance for all the wee folk!

Spirit Spirits

Choosing which spirits or facets of the divine fit into this category was not an easy task. Effectively all spirits, gods and goddesses are Spirit just by their divine or semi-divine designation. So, I decided to focus on four types of beings for this and the following two sections. First are those entities who were self-existent and self formed originators. Since Spirit is the first source to whom we seek to return, this seemed fitting.

Ao: Collective name for four chinese dragons each of whom is responsible for 1/4 of the earth.

Second are those deities who embody the inexorable power that weaves and wrangles the thread of our lives into distinct patterns, namely Fate. This takes into account those facets of the Great One who guide and bless our existence in some manner to help us achieve enlightenment. Third are beings whose essence saturates all the other elements such as the Haldde shown below. And, finally fourth are those Spirits who seem stuck in transit from one life to the next, but are nonetheless composed of that etheric essence that qualifies them for this element.

Ao: Collective name for four chinese dragons each of whom is responsible for 1/4 of the earth.

Amoghasiddhi: A Tibetan aspect of buddha who embodies spiritual perfection.

Buddha: Spiritual teacher and enlightened spirit in several different cultures of the East.

Cloud People: Pueblo ancestral spirits who live in the four corners of creation.

Duppy: Jamaican spirit that hovers near grave sights, and is most active during the in-between hours (midnight, noon).

Dybbuk: Jewish wandering spirit who can possess bodies.

Fox Fire: Germans believe this is a lost spirit, while in European tradition these are souls consigned to a type of purgatory between heaven and hell.

Gaingin: Melanesian beings who shaped all corners of creation.

Haldde (Lappish): The spirit of nature that houses portions of itself in each of the elements. Consequently we find the terms mara halddo as the sea's spirit, and cacce haldde the water's spirit.

Khmoc pray: Cambodian spirits who exist due to an untimely or violent death. These beings live in trees, and are very angry.

Lha: Pre-buddhist guardian spirits akin to angels in Tibet.

Morae (Greek): The three fates who create, measure and cut the cords of life.

Nereids: Greek catch word for all nature spirits and fairies.

Norns: Norse. The three fates.

Pretta: Hindu spirits that stay near their home for a year, especially those of children.

Resehith Hajallim: Jewish angelic spirit who grants life.

Shedu: Mesopotamian guardian spirits and intercessors, similar to guardian angels.

Winti: Guianan spirit that has no material tangibility.

Spirit Deities

Aditi: Indian Goddess who governs the past and future, whose power is inexhaustible.

Anget: Egyptian self produced goddess and giver of life. Her symbol is a cowrie shell.

Anu: Mesopotamian god who presides over fate and universal power. His symbol is a star.

Atea: Polynesian god of regenerative life force.

Baal: Canaanite god who is part of all four elements through rain, atmosphere, vegetation and the sun.

Bacabs: Mayan gods of the four winds and four directions.

Brahma: Four-headed father of the gods, the universe and men in India. His colors are red and white, and his animal is a swan.

Chiuta: African creator god who was self created and omniscient.

Chuku: Nigerian first cause. Worship him in groves of trees.

Dagda: Irish great Druid and good god, the Dagda rules over all matters of life, death and rebirth. His emblems include a wheel and an oaken harp.

Dazhbog: Slavic god who governs fair destinies.

Enlil: Sumarian god of nature's forces who keeps the Tablets of Destiny upon which the fate of even the gods themselves are written.

Fa: Benin god of destiny who can intercede for humankind (fate in this belief system is not "fixed").

Fortuna: Roman goddess who, as her name might imply, steers the fortunes of humans for boon or bane. Her emblem is a wheel.

Janus: Two-headed Roman god who represents the future and past, comings and goings, and beginnings and endings.

Jupiter: Roman god of the elements and supreme being. Offer him libations of rainwater or mead.

Hawthor: Egyptian goddess who birthed all gods and goddesses. A self-begotten being and cosmic goddess who personified nature. Her emblems include the cow, tambourine and flowers.

Hermes: Greek god of the four winds, four elements and four seasons. Appropriate emblems for him include the lyre and dice.

Iris: Greek goddess of the rainbow and messenger to the gods who also presides over telepathy. Offer her figs and honey cakes.

Ishtar: Mesopotamian goddess who mothered the gods and people, and is the guardian of order. Her emblem is an eight-pointed star, and her sacred animals include the lion and dragon.

Khepri: Egyptian transformational god of creative energy, eternal life and resurrection. His name means "always becoming."

Maat: Egyptian Goddess whose domain is the inescapable order and progress of the universe. Upon death, a soul's worthiness is weighed on a scale against a red plume from her crown.

Mammetun: Assyrian goddess of destiny.

Morgan: Irish queen of the Fairy, goddess of fate. Her animal is a raven or crow.

Mut: Egyptian self-produced goddess and world mother whose sacred animals are the cat and lion. Have a cauldron in your sacred space to honor her.

Neith: Egyptian goddess whose name means "I have come from myself." The opener of ways. Her color is red.

Nemesis: Greek goddess whose name means "the inevitable." She represents that which cannot be avoided. She will sometimes intercede on a worthy person's behalf with Fate, specifically for a longer life. Her sacred emblems are an apple, a bow and a wreath.

Ninhursag: Cymarin goddess of the creative principle and the source of all life. Decorate your sacred space with leafy branches.

Nyame: African supreme deity who plots out a person's fate and prepares the soul for birth.

Olorus: Yoruban lord of heaven who controls the elements.

Ormizd: Persian supreme master of heaven who rules over universal law, light and creation.

Ptah: Egyptian god of all beginnings. The creative power behind the gods. His symbol is the ankh.

Shiva: Hindu lord of the cosmic dance, and rhythm of the universe.

Soko: Nigerian creator god who governs the elements and rules over the dead.

Svantovitt: Four-headed Slavic god who faces all four quarters of creation and is the god of all gods. Offer him libations of wine.

Tonatiuh: Aztec ruler of fate and god of battle.

Ra: Egyptian god who is the source of all life, truth and fate. Sacred symbols include the sun, a falcon and/or a ram.

Renenet: Egyptian goddess who gave babies their names, attributes and fortunes. She is also a judge of the dead along with the God of destiny, Shai. Her sacred animals are the lion (for strength) and snake (for transformation).

Saturn: Roman father of time very similar to Cronus in Greek mythology. Saturn dispenses life's lessons.

Sin: Mesopotamian god who measures time and presides over fate.

T'ai-Yueh-Ta-Ti: Chinese god who portions out good and bad karma, and governs fate.

Tara: Tibetan Queen of Heaven and mother of buddhas, she is transcendent. Her flower is the lotus, and her colors are green and white.

Varuna: Hindu god who maintains all balance, equity and order in the universe. Lord of creative power and life force. His sacred emblem is a lasso and his animal is a white horse.

Viracocha: Incan god without beginning or end. Present him libations of rainwater.

Zurvan: Persian god of infinite space and time, having four faces corresponding to the four seasons and directions.

> **Among Hindus, the vital essence of one's soul is called *atman*.**

Correspondence List

ANIMALS & INSECTS: Any mythological, fantastic creature such as the sphinx. Those that exhibit characteristics from two or more elements including: antelope (Air/Earth), armadillo (Fire/Earth), beaver (Water/Earth), bee (Air/Fire), cardinal (Fire/Air), dragon (Fire/Air), Gull (Water/Air), elephant (Earth/Water/Fire), kowala (Earth/Air), pegasus (Earth/Air), roadrunner (Fire/Earth/Air), robin (Fire/Air), skunk (Air/Earth/Fire), and unicorn (all). Also the dove (biblical).

APPLICATIONS: Awareness, spiritual self discovery, transmutation, transcendence, integration, finding a religious path, karmic connections and impacts, your place in the greater scheme of things, awareness of the Divine within all, enlightenment, blending different facets of self (or a group) into harmonious union.

ARCHANGEL: Angel of the Presence.

ASTROLOGICAL SIGNS: All in sequence.

CELESTIAL INFLUENCE: Galaxies, what is known of the Universe, stars as sometimes representing souls, cosmic rays.

COLOR: All, but none discernable from the rest. Also brilliant white and rainbows.

CRYSTALS, METALS, STONES: Amber, Boji stones, coral, electrum, fossils, holey stones, jet, mother of pearl, petrified wood. Also, layered stones that evidence time's passage, stones with unusual inclusions and phantoms, mottled pieces.

DIRECTION: Center.

EMBLEMS: The infinity sign, blended items (like four aromas—one for each element), an underground river, Pi, sparkling white light.

FOOD ITEMS (MISC): Any item that undergoes one or more elemental process. A good example would be picking a fruit from one's garden (Earth), drying it (Air), adding it to a cake mix (Fire), and freezing it for future use (Water).

GREEK SHAPE: Dodecahedron as the mingling of all elements and the matrix of the universe.

LOCATION: Center of the Earth, or above in the heavens. All center points and circumferences. Mirror images (within and without).

MOON PHASE: Blue moon.

MOONS (Folk Names): Blood Moon (October/November) as symbolic of the spirit of life.

SEASON: The entire Wheel of the Year.

SENSE: Hearing (especially to one's inner voice).

TATTWAS SYMBOL (INDIA): Akasha—black or indigo ovoid.

TAROT EMBLEM: The Fool Card, numbered zero, the point of origin and place of all potentialities. Also the Magus who is one with Spirit, and the Hierophant who has learned the voice of nature. In some decks, the Universe card.

TIME: Infinite. Also during eclipses or when the sun and moon are seen together in the sky.

WIND (name): Aeolus (Guardian of all four winds).

Appendix
Devic Dictionary

Early in this book I mentioned that the world of Fey is quite populous and diverse. This glossary will provide you with some feeling for that variety. Note that I have chosen to list mostly "good" fairies here, as those are the ones to whom wise magical humans would go for aid anyway!

Apsares: Hindu water nymphs who inhabit rivers and pools.

Avalon: Fairy island where four Fairy Queens (for each element and corner of creation) look King Arthur after being mortally wounded.

Banshee: The wailing fairy-spirit of Ireland whose cries presage a death.

Bogie: Villainous fairies who revel in playing scary tricks on humans.

Brownie: Shaggy, tattered fairy who adopts the home,

watches it, and often helps with tasks like brewing.

Chillie Dhu: Scottish fairy who lives alone among birch branches, wearing nothing but leaves.

Coblynau: Welsh goblins of the mines who are always miming the work done, but never doing any themselves.

Daoine Sidhe: A type of Seelie Court fairy who take particular pride in their fighting abilities and games which are challenging.

Dwarf: Scandinavian earth dweller with a beard. They are known for mining metals.

Elf: Roguish fey with pointed ears and youthful, thin appearance. Frequently prefer forest living.

Fairy: General term for magical beings that live in a different type of reality that is less material than our own.

Fairy Rings: Circles of grass, tress or stones that mark an entrance to the land of Fey. If one falls asleep here, it may be for a thousand years!

Glaistig: Water fairy who is both vampirish and seducing. However, sometimes she has a special soft spot for children and the elderly, helping either if they happen to get lost in her domain.

Goblin: Small malicious thieves of the fairy world who are very temperamental.

Gremlin: An air fairy whose personality is one of chaos and mischief.

Gwragedd Annwn: Welsh water fairy who is quite beautiful, and may take a mortal husband upon occasion.

Hillmen: A frightful fairy who is most active on Lammas and Hollandtide (11/11).

Hollow Hills: One of the traditional living spaces for the fey.

Kelpie: Scottish stream fairy that tends toward an angry disposition.

Knockers: Cornish goblin who sometimes helps miners locate veins of minerals.

Kobold: German knockers who are not so helpful unless a whim strikes them.

Leprechaun: Industrious, wealthy fairy of Ireland who is always making but one shoe, not a pair. If you capture this fellow, he will lead you to his pot of gold.

Pixy: Cornish mischief makers who make bells ring on the moors, but may help humans in exchange for small gifts or acts of kindness.

Pooka: Irish fairy who often takes animal form, being both wild and playful akin to the Puck of Shakespeare.

Seelie Court: The aristocracy of Scottish fairies, these are trooping, heroic fey form whom the Tuatha de Danann originated.

Sidhe: Gaelic for fairy, meaning hill people. The Sidhe are said to love things of beauty.

Spriggan: Small, ugly, monstrous fairies believed to be the ghosts of old giants. Spriggans guard hill treasures, cause blight and bring whirlwinds.

Tuatha de Danann: A class who once ruled Ireland but were forced underground by the Milesians. Believed to be a remnant people from the magical Seelie Court.

Tylwyth Teg: Welsh fair-haired fairy known for wearing white clothing similar to the Silkies in Northern England who wear only white silk.

Will-o-the-wisp: A type of fire fairy whose history seems to begin in Roman times. Among Native Americans, this elemental is said to warn of impending danger.

Afterword

 epending on the reference book one reads, some historical texts and studies of same indicate that the Devas of lore existed anciently simply as a unique race of people. The mysterious Picts, driven out of Scotland by the Romans and Bretons, for example, could have become the "pixies." Likewise, the Fair Folk (so named for their light complexions) of this region, who lived in the hills and knew the ancient art of magic could translate into the "fairies." Theoretically, the diminutive terminology and depiction that took place over time was but one way for the Church to undermine magical traditions, and more importantly the influence Cunning Folk had with commoners.

If this historical hypothesis is true, then our mythic friends were once as vital and alive as are we. This does not detract from their potential to enhance our magic, however. As discussed in Chapter 2, thought forms held in the minds and hearts of people for hundreds of years can become viable energy sources in the Astral reality. Additionally, some of the spirits of these Fair Folk or Picts may act as guides. So, the ability to contact and learn from Devas is not curtailed by a historical reality, only changed somewhat in its perspective.

In either case, the idea presented by this hypothesis is important to our spiritual growth and understanding. Even in the modern world, one should not judge or dismiss those who seem "different" simply because we do not understand their way of life. By so doing, we may be overlooking a rare opportunity to evolve as a species. Likewise, magical ways and history should not be left idle on a dusty bookshelf. Reclaim them, and make them live again. Dance with the fairies, dream with the Unicorns, Draw down the moon, and be blessed.

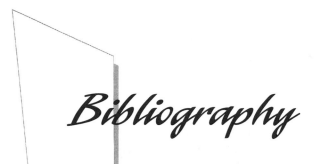

Bibliography

Adams, Ruth & Hutchinson, Ruth *Every Day's a Holiday*
Harper & Row, NYC, 1951

Arrowsmith, Nancy *Field Guide to the Little People*
Pocket Books, NYC, 1977

Baumgartner, Anne S. *Complete Dictionary of the Gods*
University Books, NYC, 1984

Briggs, Katharine *An Encyclopedia of Fairies*
Pantheon Books, NYC, 1976

Budapest, Z.E. *Grandmother of Time*
HarperCollins, NYC, 1989

Carlyon, Richard *A Guide to the Gods*
Wm. Morrow & Co., NYC, 1982

Chaundler, Christine *Everyman's Book of Superstition*
Philosophical Library, NYC, 1970

Clarkson, Rosetta *Green Enchantment*
Macmillan, NYC, 1940

Conway, D.J. *Ancient & Shining Ones*
Llewellyn Publications, St. Paul, MN, 1993

Cotterell, Authur ed. *Macmillan Illustrated
Encyclopedia of Myth and Legend*
Macmillan, NYC, 1989

Cunningham, Scott
Encyclopedia of Crystal, Gem and Metal Magic
Llewellyn Publications, St. Paul, MN, 1988
Earth Power
Llewellyn Publications, St. Paul, MN, 1983
Magical Herbalism
Llewellyn Publications, St. Paul, MN, 1985
The Magic in Food
Llewellyn Publications, St. Paul MN, 1990

Farpid, B. & Lee, A. ***Fairies***
Souvenir Press, NYC, 1978

Farrar, Janet & Stewart
The Witches' Goddess
Phoenix Publishing, Custer, WA, 1987
The Witches' God
Phoenix Publishing, WA,1989

Felding, William J. ***Strange Superstitions
and Magical Practices***
Paperback Library, NYC, 1968

Hall, Manley P. ***The Secret Teachings of All Ages***
Philosophical Research Society, Los Angeles, CA 1977

Kunz, G.F. ***The Curious Lore of Precious Stones***
Dover Publications, NYC, 1913

Lasne, Sophie & Gaultier, A.P. ***Dictionary of Superstitions***
Prentice Hall, NJ, 1984

Leach, Maria, ed. ***Standard Dictionary of Folklore,
Mythology and Legend***
Funk & Wagnall, NYC, 1972

Lorie, Peter ***Superstitions***
Simon & Schuster, NYC, 1992

Mercatante, A.S. *Zoo of the Gods*
Harper & Row, NYC, 1974

Murphy, Richard & Appenzeller, Tim, eds. *Fairies & Elves*
Time Life Books, VA, 1984

New Larousse Encyclopedia of Mythology
Hamlyn House, Middlesex, England, 1959

O'Hara, G. *Moonlore*
Llewellyn Publications, St. Paul, MN, 1996

Scott, Rev. J. Loughran *Bullfinch's Age of Fable*
David McKay, Philadelphia, PA, 1898

Starhawk *The Spiral Dance*
Harper & Row, NYC, 1989

Telesco, Patricia
Folkways:Reclaiming the Magic & Wisdom
Llewellyn Publications, St. Paul, MN, 1995
Kitchen Witch's Cookbook
Llewellyn Publications, St. Paul, MN, 1994
Seasons of the Sun
Samuel Weiser Inc., York Beach, ME, 1996
Witch's Brew
Llewellyn Publications, St. Paul, MN, 1995

Valiente, Doreen *Natural Magic*
Phoenix Publishing, Custer, WA, 1985

Walker, Barbara
Woman's Dictionary of Symbols and Sacred Objects
Harper & Row, CA, 1988

Suggested Reading List

For those readers who may be new to magic, the New Age, and metaphysical procedures, the following books offer solid information to get you started safely and wisely. If you have any questions on the points brought up in this primer, these books will help fill in the gaps in ways I could not in a format such as this one.

Drawing Down the Moon by Margot Adler,
Beacon Press, Boston, MA.
A book examining the modern neo-pagan movement
from a historical and sociological perspective.

Earth Magic by Marion Weinstein,
Phoenix Publishing, Custer, WA. Also
Positive Magic.
Two excellent and down-to-earth books that discuss
ritual, beliefs and practices among modern witches.

Secret Teachings of All Ages by Manley P. Hall,
Philosophical Research Society, Los Angeles, CA.
A scholarly approach to metaphysical ideals evidenced at
various junctures in history, within different cultural contexts.
Heavy reading, but a superb resource.

Spinning Spells; Weaving Wonders by Patricia Telesco,
Crossing Press, CA.
A how-to book for creative spellcraft using components
readily found in and around the sacred space of home.

Spiral Dance by Starhawk,
Harper & Row, San Francisco, CA.
An excellent guide to rituals through the year.

Urban Pagan by Patricia Telesco,
Llewellyn Publications, St. Paul, MN.
Especially suited to those readers who live in
a city environment.

WitchCraft Today by Scott Cunningham,
Llewellyn Publications, St. Paul, MN.
Any books by Cunningham are very approachable and
understandable. This one in particular tackles questions
about what Wicca is, and is not, in the modern world.

The Amityville Horror Conspiracy

by Stephen Kaplan, Ph.D., and
Roxanne Salch Kaplan

$14.95*

Paperback- 6"x9"
240 pages

Now Available From

Belfry Books

Available at your local bookstore or order direct from publisher—

One of the biggest stories of the 20th century, the "Amityville Horror" began with the killing of the DeFeo family by one of their own—the "Horror House" was sold to the Lutz family, who after only two weeks fled from the demonic forces tormenting them…Did hellish creatures cross the barrier between worlds? The answers are frightening, frustrating, furious, and funny—but always fascinating.

"Stephen Kaplan…knows a thing or two about things that go bump in the night."—American Teacher Magazine

* Add $1.55 per book
for shipping & handling

**Canadian prices slightly higher.
Contact publisher for pricing.**

Belfry Books, a division of Toad Hall, Inc.
Rural Route 2 Box 16-B
Laceyville, PA 18623
Phone 717 869-2942
FAX 717 869-1031

Now Available From

 Belfry Books

$14.95*

Paperback- 6"x9"
208 pages

"Never Cross a Palm With Silver"
—by Jacqueline Lichtenberg

Jacqueline is a renowned esoteric scholar, astrologer, Tarot expert, novelist, critic and teacher. This is the first book in a controversial new series that looks at the Biblical origins of the Tarot.

Explore these fascinating ideas!
- **What the Bible really has to say about divination.**
- **How and why the Kabbala (the Jewish mystery school) and the Tarot are intertwined.**
- **What Moses has to do with the Tarot.**
- **Why Jesus most likely studied the Tarot.**

* Add $1.55 per book
for shipping & handling

**Canadian prices slightly higher.
Contact publisher for pricing.**

Belfry Books, A division of Toad Hall, Inc.
Rural Route 2 Box 16-B
Laceyville, PA 18623
Phone 717 869-2942
FAX 717 869-1031

Now available from ![Belfry Books logo] Belfry Books

Teachings of the Winged Disk

by Phaedron∴

Hierophant, Holy Order of the Winged Disk

$14.95*

Paperback- 6"x9"
224 pages

Now it is possible to be at one with the universe. Hidden ways and mystical means—these are the ancient teachings of a Hermetical order—formerly passed down verbally from Adept to student. Egyptian, Qabalistic, alchemical, Hermetic, Gnostic Rosicrucian…a blending of awesome knowledge, creating a serious spiritual path to Magickal experiences, mastery of self and surroundings, and unveiling the secrets of the cosmos.

"This is what every occult student should know."
—V.H. Fra. P.C.A. Hermetic Order of the
Eternal Golden Dawn International

Available at your local bookstore
or order direct from publisher—

* Add $1.55 per book
for shipping & handling

Canadian prices slightly higher.
Contact publisher for pricing.

Belfry Books, a division of Toad Hall, Inc.
Rural Route 2 Box 16-B
Laceyville, PA 18623
Phone 717 869-2942
FAX 717 869-1031